Special Education Law Case Studies

Special Education Law Case Studies

A Review from Practitioners

David Bateman and Jenifer Cline
with Jonathan Steele and Sean Fields

ROWMAN & LITTLEFIELD
Lanham • Boulder • New York • London

Published by Rowman & Littlefield
An imprint of The Rowman & Littlefield Publishing Group, Inc.
4501 Forbes Boulevard, Suite 200, Lanham, Maryland 20706
www.rowman.com

6 Tinworth Street, London SE11 5AL

Distributed by NATIONAL BOOK NETWORK

British Library Cataloguing in Publication Information Available

Library of Congress Cataloging-in-Publication Data

Names: Bateman, David, 1963- author. | Cline, Jenifer L., author. | Steele,
    Jonathan D., author. | Fields, Sean A., author.
Title: Special education law case studies : a review from practitioners /
    David Bateman and Jenifer Cline with Jonathan Steele and Sean Fields.
Description: Lanham : Rowman & Littlefield, 2019.
Identifiers: LCCN 2018043768 (print) | LCCN 2018044313 (ebook) | ISBN
    9781475837698 (e-book) | ISBN 9781475837674 (hardcover) | ISBN
    9781475837681 (paperback)
Subjects: LCSH: Special education—Law and legislation—United States—Case
    studies.
Classification: LCC KF4209.3 (ebook) | LCC KF4209.3 .B374 2019 (print) | DDC
    344.73/0791—dc23
LC record available at https://lccn.loc.gov/2018043768

∞™ The paper used in this publication meets the minimum requirements of
American National Standard for Information Sciences—Permanence of Paper
for Printed Library Materials, ANSI/NISO Z39.48-1992.

Printed in the United States of America

Contents

Preface   vii

Introduction   ix

Case One: Sarah   1
    Private School and a Free Appropriate Public Education

Case Two: Josh   12
    Extended School Year Eligibility

Case Three: Calvin   22
    Behavioral Issues

Case Four: Manuel   30
    Least Restrictive Environment

Case Five: Sawyer   38
    Assistive Technology

Case Six: Caleb   47
    Identification and Changing Schools

Case Seven: Bryson   53
    IEP Implementation

Case Eight: Conner   61
    Communication with School

Case Nine: Layla   69
    Behavioral Issues

Case Ten: Nolan   77
    Compensatory Education

Case Eleven: Zander   85
    Autism/Behavioral Issues

Case Twelve: Mason   92
    Mediation Order Implementation

Case Thirteen: Brody   100
    Child Find

Case Fourteen: Destiny   110
    Section 504

Case Fifteen: Amelia   119
    Compensatory Education

About the Authors   129

Preface

Case studies are a helpful way to understand difficult issues. The case studies presented here are of actual students eligible for special education and related services. The names and a few slight facts were changed to preserve confidentiality.

The case studies are represented not to tell districts and parents that this is the only way questions about special education law can be answered, but to provide likely answers along with commentary for analysis. Please consult an attorney in your state for specific answers to legal questions.

Introduction

Each year, hundreds of school districts appoint leaders responsible for general and special education. These leaders could be responsible for all of the education needs of the district, or for a certain age range of students, or a certain number of schools, or even certain types of disabilities. Each, however, is charged with making sure students eligible for special education and related services receive a free appropriate public education, as they are entitled to. These leaders oversee departments and play important roles in the leadership of the district.

Many leaders have worked for years as either teachers or related services providers, and most states have standards for certification for the role of the I administrator/leader. With their broad formal education and years of experience, they should be able to meet the challenges of building and leading programs. Education leaders need to be prepared to tackle any problem related to teaching and learning, personnel selection and evaluation, basic financial management, and parent and community relations. This also includes the many legal demands related to special education. However, just like other school leaders, many education leaders are overwhelmed with the demands of the job while at the same time having to provide services to an increasingly diverse population in an underfunded system and deal with a growing negative public perception of the education system.

Many leaders will experience the burden of many responsibilities in their position, such as fulfilling the spirit and letter of the law regarding students with disabilities, helping staff keep abreast of best practices, and meeting the ever-increasing demands from communities and families. They will suddenly be thrust into situations in which they must become the final arbiter on matters related to the plethora of processes and procedures such as IEP team meetings, manifestation determinations, requests for mediation or due process hearings, and IDEA compliance. It is likely that many of these individuals will be new leaders who will need guidance and direction as they move their teams ahead. Additionally, services for students with disabilities are nuanced and increasingly litigious.

BACKGROUND

Tremendous changes have occurred over the past decade in the provision of services to students with disabilities. Federal mandates continue to define requirements for a free appropriate public education (FAPE) in the least restrictive environment. Additionally, there has been an increase in the number of lawsuits filed against school districts regarding the provision of educational services for students with disabilities. The present climate of school restructuring is placing new leadership demands on all leaders, including those responsible for students with disabilities. Furthermore, the move toward education in more inclusive settings necessitates shared responsibility and schoolwide collaboration among supervisors, principals, general and special education teachers, and related service personnel. To be effective, today's special education leaders must be knowledgeable about programs for students with disabilities and educational standards for general education classes, and must provide appropriate support to teachers. They must work to ensure that special education is integrated into the general program and that the multiple programs offered within a school system work to benefit all students.

Knowledge is critical in working with students with disabilities. Many parents have diligently studied federal and state laws and court decisions. They are skilled at using legal language to influence decisions in their favor. It is critical that special education school leaders have a resource that guides them to build relationships and to work successfully with parents to help meet the needs of students. Likewise, with the expectation that students receiving special education will access the general education curriculum, school leaders need to confidently guide teachers in providing appropriate education to students with disabilities, and to find ways of working with parents to prevent short- and long-term problems.

Recognizing that few leaders feel adequately prepared for these new roles, *Special Education Law Case Studies* was developed to enable practicing administrators to understand and apply the details of special education law.

Effective implementation of special education in any district relies on a solid understanding of the rules and regulations governing special education. In this book we enumerate key laws, as promulgated by the federal government, that influence special education, such as the Individuals with

Disabilities Education Act and Section 504 of the Vocational Rehabilitation Act of 1973.

Litigation affects the implementation of regulations. There is probably a specific case affecting the implementation of special education in just about every district. The cases will be tied to the main principles of the law to aid in not only understanding the law, but also in helping leaders and teachers realize the nuances of the law for students with disabilities.

CASES

Using cases for instruction has many advantages. First, readers are forced to engage in the details and absorb the information to render a decision and to determine how to move forward. Second, though rulings will be described as a part of the decision for the case, there is often ambiguity when dealing with special education law. We provide the reader with helpful steps to consider moving forward, no matter the situation. Third, cases, as we present them, allow for self-paced learning, where an individual can move forward as quickly or slowly as they wish. Fourth, it is important to learn that although hearing officer decisions will be provided, the best step is to look for ways to move forward that help everyone—the student, the family, the teachers, and the administrators.

THE CASES

The cases are designed to present an overview of the law from both areas where there is frequent litigation and from traditional categorical areas. Using cases to understand legal issues is not new. Law schools assign students readings from many cases. This will build on that logic but work to improve the methodology. Specifically, the cases in this book are ones school leaders and teachers can relate to, and may have experienced. There have been multiple lawsuits that have been adjudicated by the Supreme Court, and yes, they are very important. However, the vast majority of cases involving special education are cases heard by an impartial due process hearing officer. There are grey areas. There may be implementation issues. There are often disputes regarding what is appropriate.

The cases present enough information for the reader to understand the intricacies of the situation and then ask specific questions about the ruling. Each case then presents information from a special education administrator about what can be learned from the case in order to guide the district in helping not only the student and family, but also the teachers moving forward. Next is commentary from an attorney who frequently represents school districts in special education litigation. This commentary will provide a legal perspective about how to help the district move forward. The commentaries may overlap, but we feel it is important to provide guidance on the specifics and the different ways each professional will look at the situation. Finally, we present commentary from an attorney who solely represents parents in due process hearings. It is important to get all perspectives in order to understand the issues.

It is important to point out that the value of analyzing cases is to enhance practical knowledge of leadership in schools while simultaneously strengthening problem-solving. Understanding research is very important, but understanding the implications of the law for students with disabilities is also crucial. The cases present real-life situations, and the hope is that the reader will use the information with the intention of making decisions and learning from others.

The cases were developed to help new (and experienced) special education leaders and supervisors survive the pressures of working with students with disabilities while working to provide appropriate services and prevent litigation. Many texts are filled with theories, but very little practical advice has been available specifically about day-to-day operations. This book is organized to give new special education leaders that practical advice. The information contained here offers answers to many of the problems special education leaders face relating to students with disabilities.

Case One: Sarah

Private School and a Free Appropriate Public Education

DUE PROCESS PROCEDURE

The following is a summary of the background of the case, the school district's position, the family's position, and the hearing officer's findings.

BACKGROUND

Sarah is a fifteen-year-old ninth grade student who is eligible for special education and related services and is currently attending an out-of-state private school. There is no dispute she is eligible for special education as a student with a specific learning disability.

During her seventh-grade year, Sarah was doing well academically but began to show signs of self-injurious behaviors such as cutting herself. The individualized education program (IEP) written during her seventh-grade year did not include any services to address behavioral concerns. These behaviors continued and escalated to the level of requiring psychiatric hospitalization during eighth grade. She was hospitalized due to depression, self-harming, hallucinations, and post-traumatic stress disorder. The school district was aware of her behaviors and the frequent psychiatric hospitalizations. Sarah also made numerous visits to the nurse's office during seventh and eighth grade; sometimes multiple trips would occur in a day.

The district believed Sarah's psychiatric placements in the spring of her eighth-grade year impacted her academic progress, and therefore resulted in intermittent academic work and a modification of the traditional letter grading method, assigning pass/fail grades. Sarah did not return to school after March 15 of that year. At the end of eighth grade, the district did discuss the need for Sarah to receive instruction in the home, which would focus on the eighth-grade information and concepts missed from January to June. Instead of participating in the instruction in the home, the parents enrolled her in an out-of-state private school. Sarah continued to be treated by an out-of-school psychiatric facility for her emotional issues. Sarah's parents sent a written request to the school district for an IEP meeting during that spring. An IEP meeting was held in June. During that meeting Sarah was found not eligible for extended school year (ESY). The IEP did not include any information as to how the team made that determination. Also, during this meeting the district stated Sarah's psychiatric placements impacted her educational progress. However, there was no baseline data against which to measure identified goals, nor did the goals address her emotional needs.

The parents informed the district of the private school summer placement in which Sarah was receiving primarily remedial courses to make up for the work missed during the spring of eighth grade. Upon receipt of this information, the district did not initiate any further action.

QUESTIONS TO BE ANSWERED BY THE HEARING OFFICER

1. Was the Student offered FAPE during the seventh and eighth grades?
2. Did the IEP offered in June of eighth grade provide her FAPE?
3. Is her placement at the private school for ninth grade an appropriate placement?
4. Is the student entitled to tuition reimbursement for placement at the private school for ninth grade as well as for ESY placement during the summer after eighth grade?
5. Is the student entitled to any compensatory education due to FAPE not being provided during seventh and eighth grade?

PARENTS' POSITION

The parents believe the district IEP failed to provide FAPE for the seventh and eighth grade school years. They also believe the district should pay for summer programming and tuition at the private school for the ninth-grade year.

Sarah's parents believe the district should have convened an IEP meeting during the spring of eighth grade and revised the IEP to provide educational services in accordance with her then current special needs. The parents believe that in not doing so, the district failed to provide FAPE. The parents requested reimbursement of costs associated with Sarah's programming provided in the summer after eighth grade, which the parents secured to re-mediate the missed education and learning that occurred the previous spring.

The parents believe the record clearly indicates Sarah had an extensive history of educational and psychiatric needs. The parents, undisputedly, were in constant contact with district staff concerning traumatic events in Sarah's life. When the IEP team convened in June to develop an IEP for Sarah's ninth-grade year, the district was acutely aware of the series of psychiatric placements that were incurred during the spring semester of her eighth-grade year. The parents believe the IEP developed in June did not address her social-emotional needs and considered how these needs might impact her academic achievement in the coming school year. The parents went on to claim that all of Sarah's placements, both in-patient and partial hospitalization, were known and accessible to the district. Yet the district never sought to convene an IEP meeting to revise the IEP to reflect Sarah's current needs and situation.

The parents went on to state the fact the district not having day-to-day, in-school access to the child was not a free pass to disregard the responsibility to provide FAPE. The district did make an effort to provide for Sarah during the time she was in school during that semester. However, no action was taken to address her emotional needs. The record indicates that when one of the program representatives endeavored to coordinate Sarah's program to provide emotional support services in the school setting, the school failed to either coordinate with the provider or revise the IEP and provide the services themselves.

DISTRICT POSITION

The district shared that, even though they were aware of her in-patient psychiatric placements, the behaviors prompting these placements were not evidenced in the school setting. They also shared that the determination of the reasonableness and appropriateness of an IEP is assessed by the IEP team using the information available to the team at the time of the meeting. They did not identify her in seventh grade or the first part of eighth grade as a student with emotional difficulties, because she was not demonstrating those behaviors in school. The district went on to state that, notwithstanding all of Sarah's in-patient and partial hospitalization placements, she was doing fine while she was in school. Accordingly, they stated, Sarah was not identifiable as emotionally disturbed. The district's school psychologist stated that an in-patient hospitalization for psychiatric treatment would impact a student's education, and clarified that when cognizant of a student having been in psychiatric placements, the psychologist should request reports concerning these placements as part of the IEP development process. The district stated they did not seek the records because they did not see emotional problems in school, even though they were aware of her placements in psychiatric facilities. At the time of the IEP meeting in June after eighth grade, Sarah had not been in school since March 15, and the staff were aware of the reasons for her absence. They also stated that tuition reimbursement was not warranted, because they could provide an appropriate education for her based on their June IEP.

DECISION

The hearing officer found the record replete with evidence and testimony that, between January and June of eighth grade, the district knew Sarah was suffering academically as well as emotionally, and the district had a legal obligation, pursuant to IDEA, to convene an IEP meeting, even before the parents requested one.

The hearing officer also held that the IEP developed in June did not appropriately address Sarah's needs for her ninth-grade school year. The litany of psychiatric placements in the spring of eighth grade should have compelled the IEP team to consider any anticipated needs due to these placements. Further, the record amply supported that Sarah's psychiatric placements in the spring of eighth grade had an impact on her grades.

The claim that the school district did not have a responsibility toward a student who was not demonstrating problems in school was refuted by the hearing officer. The hearing officer stated that the student's needs cannot be compartmentalized and should at least be considered by the IEP team. Finally, the hearing officer supported the notion that Sarah should have been identified as emotionally disturbed during the spring semester of eighth grade, if not sooner. The hearing officer found a denial of FAPE by the district during spring of eighth grade, and found that compensatory education is appropriate such that Sarah is entitled to receive the programming, which the district failed to provide.

Compensatory Education

Compensatory education is an in-kind remedy designed to provide eligible students with the services they should have received pursuant to FAPE. A student receiving special education services is entitled to compensatory educational services if through some action or inaction of the district the student was denied FAPE. The hearing officer is obligated to determine if the program and placement offered by the district meet the procedural requirements of IDEA and are reasonably calculated to confer meaningful educational benefit. The standard of "reasonably calculated to confer meaningful educational benefit" means the IEP is based on a thorough evaluation and addresses all of the child's needs. The plain language of IDEA and the *Endrew F.* decision speak clearly to this issue. Thus, a district is obligated to provide compensatory education when it fails to provide FAPE to an eligible student.

The hearing officer also awarded the parents the tuition reimbursement sought for the summer programming, despite the district offering tutoring services over the summer to remediate programming lost. The district failed to fulfill its promise in providing appropriate services to the student. As such, the parents enrolled Sarah in specialized programming at a private facility and are entitled to reimbursement of the tuition paid.

ORDER

1. The student was not offered FAPE during the spring of her eighth-grade year or awarded compensatory education based on the number of hours she was to be provided an education during that period.
2. The student was not offered FAPE for ninth grade based on the June IEP.
3. The student's placement at the private school for ninth grade constitutes an appropriate placement for her.
4. The student is entitled to tuition reimbursement for her ninth-grade year at the private school.
5. Whereas the district failed to provide her with FAPE during the period between January and June of her eighth-grade year; the parents are entitled to reimbursement of costs paid in association with the private school remedial programming they provided for her during the summer after eighth grade.

SARAH: SPECIAL EDUCATION ADMINISTRATOR RESPONSE

Sarah's case identifies multiple process issues the district needed to address:

1. Addressing in the IEP how the disability was negatively impacting her education—time out of class
2. Not conducting an IEP meeting in a timely manner when requested by the parents
3. Not considering information from outside service providers when proposing a program for Sarah's education

4. Not gathering baseline data for the goals in the IEP, and not developing goals to address her emotional needs
5. Not promptly providing tuition reimbursement and compensatory educational services

The errors within these areas led to the conclusion by the hearing officer that Sarah did not receive FAPE during the time in question, which resulted in awarding Sarah compensatory educational services.

Appropriate IEP Services

This case reflects a matter schools often face: a disability not overtly manifesting at school but still negatively impacting the student's education. Her poor attendance and time in the nurse's office did not allow Sarah to access her education. School teams consider attendance when evaluating if a disability is adversely impacting a student's education. However, in this case they failed to consider that the frequent trips to the nurse's office did not qualify as "attendance." Even though Sarah was in school, her trips to the nurse's office were impacting her participating in her education because she was not in the classroom. Even though she was not demonstrating the behaviors at school, treatment for those behaviors was interfering, and therefore should have been addressed by the IEP team. Schools need to be aware of and consider the impacts of a disability that may not be directly impacting the student in school, but may have a secondary impact. With the school's knowledge of Sarah's self-harming behaviors, there should have been some actions taken as soon as she began to make frequent visits to the nurse's office complaining of stomach pain and headaches. As discussed in the case, the school was obligated to consider if any changes needed to be made to the program to address Sarah's trips to the nurse's office and her absences due to admission to treatment facilities. It is important to consider how much instruction a student is missing. In this case Sarah's absences escalated from multiple trips to the nurse's office to significant absences, and therefore Sarah was denied FAPE. Poor attendance does not allow a student to access their education, even if their grades are all right.

Holding an IEP Meeting in a Timely Manner

The second mistake the school district made was not having an IEP meeting shortly after the parents requested it. This case does not give us the details as to why the meeting was not held until June and when exactly the request was made. However, IDEA gives the parents the right to a timely response to any reasonable request. The IEP is one of the most important pieces of special education. It lays the foundation and outlines a plan that will ensure a student is receiving FAPE. An IEP can change at any time to reflect changes in order to meet the student's need in their current situation. Any of the team members can call an IEP meeting and one should be called when the program is not meeting the student's current needs. When an IEP team meeting is requested, it needs to be taken very seriously and acted upon as soon as possible. This team should have reconvened in the spring instead of waiting until June to figure out how to allow Sarah access to her education, even though she was not at school. The IDEA gives parents the right to request a meeting and to have action taken on it in a reasonable amount of time.

Outside Service Provider Information

There is no requirement that the district "request the records" from an outside agency; however, by not doing so, the team did not demonstrate a good faith effort to develop an appropriate program by not even considering information from outside agencies. When the family informed the district of the placements, they should have attempted to gather the information so that the team could "consider" it. That information may have included strategies Sarah was being taught to deal with her anxiety. It also may have led the team to some teaching strategies, accommodation, or modifications that would have been appropriate to use in the school setting. Making sure that an educational team has all of the appropriate information before making programming decisions is just good practice.

IEP Development

When an IEP is not meeting a student's needs, the team needs to reconvene to make needed adjustments. Even though the parents requested an IEP team meeting in the spring, it was not held until June. The IEP proposed in June did not address social-emotional needs or include baseline data on Sarah's level of achievement. When reflecting on the situation, it can be shown that the disability that was causing Sarah to miss so much class time, even when she was at school, needed to be addressed in the IEP. The goal of special education is to get students to a level that they no longer need the service. This goal cannot be reached if all of the factors inhibiting progress are not considered and addressed. In this case, Sarah was not coming to school due to mental health needs. The district did not consider qualifying her under another label; students can and do have multiple qualification categories. IDEA states that the IEP must have academic and/or functional goals designed to "(A) Meet the child's needs that result from the child's disability to enable to child to be involved in and make progress in the general curriculum; and (B) Meet each of the child's other educational needs that result from the child's disability" [§300.320(a)(2)(i), (A)(B)]. Sarah was demonstrating a need to increase her attendance or gain access to the education in an alternate mode, as well as learn and use coping strategies. The school could have supported her mental health goals while providing her FAPE.

IDEA requires a student's IEP to include a description of the students "present level of academic achievement and functional performance" [§300.320(a) (1)], including "How the child's disability affects the child's involvement and progress in the general educational curriculum" [§300.320(a)(1)(i)]. Understandably, this would have been difficult to get since the student was not attending school at the time. However, the school could and should have gone to her and gathered some baseline data. Without that baseline data, future education planning is a "shot in the dark." The team may have been able to use some the data included in the outside reports that they did not request.

When all of these factors are considered, the conclusion that Sarah did not receive FAPE and therefore compensatory education is appropriate.

Tuition and Compensatory Educational Services

Finally, IDEA states that

> If the parents of a child with a disability, who previously received special education and related services under the authority of public agency, enroll the child in a private preschool, elementary school, or secondary school without the consent of or referral by the public agency, a court or a hearing officer my require the agency to reimburse the parents for the cost of that enrollment if the court or hearing officer finds that the agency had not made FAPE available to the child in a timely manner prior to that enrollment and that the private placement is appropriate. [§300.148(c)]

This clearly describes the situation regarding Sarah's education.

The private school Sarah's parents chose was able to meet all of her needs, emotional and educational. Since the district did not respond to the family in a timely manner when Sarah's problems were escalating and there were increasing problems with her attendance, tuition payment by the district is appropriate. Every eligible child is due a free appropriate public education. Despite the fact Sarah had received intermittent educational opportunities and the district offered her a plan, outlined in the IEP, it was not enough to allow her to have access to and progress in the general curriculum. Therefore, FAPE was denied.

One of the foundations of our country is the belief that all citizens have the right to be educated. Although there is no mention of education in the U.S. Constitution, states took on the responsibility of educating youth. Since then, civil rights laws that prevent discrimination have included education. This is where the term "free appropriate public education" was born. If states were going to provide education, they could not withhold education from students with disabilities. Students should be able to reap the benefits of an education for their own purpose. Therefore, one can think of FAPE as a property right. In this case, Sarah was denied her property right of education and therefore was awarded compensatory education and tuition reimbursement for the time she was not receiving that education.

SARAH: SCHOOL DISTRICT ATTORNEY RESPONSE

There were a number of facts provided in this case study that would concern me if I were representing this school district. One major oversight was the failure to evaluate Sarah for behavioral issues based on the early warning signs. Being hospitalized three times in seventh grade should have raised some red flags. Additionally, the repeated trips to the nurse's office were a warning sign that undermines an argument that signs of psychological or behavioral issues were only occurring outside of school. Districts should document school attendance and should be documenting trips to the nurse's office and considering this time away from the classroom as an area of concern. Therefore, the psychological and behavioral issues that were occurring were not taking place in a vacuum.

While districts don't always know everything that might be going on in a student's life, when facts like multiple hospitalizations present themselves, it becomes very hard for the attorney representing the district to argue that the district adequately followed its obligation to identify and evaluate the student for issues that might require substantial changes to the student's IEP. These issues should be prompts to considering evaluations based on the individual events and the repetition of those events.

A student's failure to return to school after March 15, in the eighth grade raises a major concern regarding whether the student is receiving FAPE, and should be followed by an assessment of additional services that might be warranted. The district should have convened the IEP team prior to the student being provided home instruction, because it could be found to be a change in placement without any evaluation of whether there were more recent issues to address and which service would best address those issues.

One mistake districts sometimes make is to fall into the trap of not paying enough attention to new issues that may arise in students who have an IEP, especially when those students are not at school for a particular period of time. This is the "out of sight, out of mind" problem that is not unusual when a student with an IEP is either receiving instruction in the home or at a private school. Public schools sometimes lose sight of the fact that they are still the responsible local educational agency (LEA) and cannot afford to forget about those students.

Despite my criticism of the school district's response, I am a little baffled by the award of tuition reimbursement for the ninth-grade year based on the number of hours the student was denied FAPE. If the hearing officer determined that FAPE was not being provided in eighth grade, I would be very curious to see how the specific number of hours was calculated in a manner to constitute a total that warrants an entire year of tuition reimbursement. Additionally, while compensatory education is a remedy that focuses on a district's sins of the past, I am not sure what the rationale was awarding full tuition rather than the cost for remedial programming.

SARAH: PARENT ATTORNEY RESPONSE

Sarah's case presents a common scenario shared by parents who contact our office. Their child's emotional and behavioral needs have taken over the home. The family reaches out to any potential source for help. When they report the concerns to the school, the LEA brushes it off and says they don't see it so there is nothing they can do. Thus, the parent continues to search for help. An attorney is rarely at the top of the list for help, but we are on the list.

It is difficult to imagine a scenario where admission to a psychiatric treatment facility does not impact a child's education. Here, Sarah's needs were preventing her from accessing an education. She frequently went to the nurse's office and missed considerable education while she was seeking mental health treatment. We should all recognize this as impacting her education and signaling a need for intervention. Despite clear and consistent case law that LEAs need to address all areas of education, including social and emotional needs, the focus remains largely on academics. As one court put it:

> Courts have been clear that emotional issues which occur at home are still relevant to IDEA analysis "so long as those problems had a significant effect on her ability to learn." Put another way, the fact that outbursts occurred at home does not in and of itself deprive those outbursts of relevance; the question is whether the outbursts adversely affected her educational performance.[1]

---

1. *G.H. v. Great Valley Sch. Dist.*, 2013 WL 2156011, at *6 (E.D. Pa. May 20, 2013) [citing *Muller v. Comm.* on Special Educ., 145 F.3d 95, 102 (2nd Cir. 1997)].

This is often the case because the LEA staff members the parents contact with their concerns are not trained to address nonacademic needs. Administrators typically serve as the complaint department. All too often, the complaint department doesn't reach out to the adults interacting with the children during the school day.

An LEA's multidisciplinary team is like the Avengers. Each member has his or her own skills and expertise, but each needs the other members to be truly effective. I am sure the school nurse recognized Sarah's symptoms signaled an emotional need. Had the nurse talked with the school social worker, I have to believe they would have created an effective plan. In order to have a team as cohesive as the Avengers, I imagine they need to meet more than once a year.

Parent attorneys have the benefit of examining the educational records and positions of the parties at one time, often after the fact. By examining every aspect of the child's education to search for a claim, we are able to make connections that may have been more difficult to see in the moment. Evidence of frequent nurse visits, a child in distress, consistent reporting by parents, poor documentation by the LEA, and no IEP changes stand out in a record review. Under a known standard (or one that should be known), a hearing officer will find that the LEA as a whole had knowledge of each of these items, even if the individuals didn't communicate with each other. An LEA can avoid this by calling for more frequent IEP meetings, but they rarely do.

As a parent attorney, I was not surprised to see a lack of documentation, a failure to reconvene the IEP team, and an LEA's resistance to consider the full impact of reported "out-of-school" concerns. These common mistakes resulted in a costly decision for the district.

Case Two: Josh

Extended School Year Eligibility

BACKGROUND

Josh is a twelve-year-old boy eligible for special education and related services as a student with an intellectual disability. He has been a resident of the district throughout his educational career. There has been a history of behavioral issues and Josh has received speech and language services in addition to his special education services. During his fourth- and fifth-grade years he received special education and related services about 75 percent of the time in a special education classroom for students with intellectual disabilities, and spent about 25 percent of his time in activities with his general education classmates. He did not make much progress on his goals and objectives that were included in his IEP, and many of the goals in fourth grade were the same goals for fifth grade.

In the spring of fifth grade, the district conducted a reevaluation and developed a new IEP for the end of fifth grade and for the beginning of sixth grade. The reevaluation did not include a functional behavior assessment or an assessment of speech and language skills.

There has been no dispute as to whether he is eligible; however, there is some dispute about whether he needs extended school year services in order to continue his progress in the curriculum.

QUESTIONS TO BE ANSWERED BY THE HEARING OFFICER

The hearing officer was obligated to determine if the program and placement offered by the district met the procedural requirements of IDEA and were reasonably calculated.

PARENTS' POSITION

The parents stated that Josh's programming for the summer after fifth grade did not describe the services or interventions to be provided during the four-week program of fifteen hours per week, nor did the extended school year (ESY) instructor review Josh's then current IEP prior to or during the period in which she provided services. The ESY teacher's information about what should be provided to Josh came from a conversation with the student's previous year teacher.

The parents stated that in the IEP developed for the end of the fifth-grade year, the team had again indicated Josh engaged in behaviors that impeded his learning and that of his peers, but again conducted no functional behavior assessment (or any other systematic behavioral assessment) or behavior intervention plan. The parents stated that again the district conducted no assessment of speech and language skills, or a functional or other systematic behavior assessment. The district created no behavior intervention plan. The IEP was based, in part, on a missing evaluation authored by Josh's special education teacher. The IEP team met and created an IEP before the reevaluation was complete.

The parents went on to state that the district did not conduct an evaluation to determine Josh's needs in speech and language, although the district agreed he had needs in that area since it included speech and language goals in the IEP.

There is no dispute that the IEP includes goals and instruction in speech and language. Therefore, the parents state that the IEP team has determined that Josh has difficulties in speech and language and needs services. However, the parents state that the district asserts there is no reason to evaluate and determine the basis for the speech needs. The parents allege the program and placement offered by the district does not meet the procedural requirements of IDEA and are reasonably calculated to confer meaningful educational benefit. [See *Board of Education v. Rowley*, 458 U.S. 176, 102 S. Ct. 3034 (1982).]

Specifically, the parents allege in their complaint that the district denied FAPE to Josh by:

a) failing to re-evaluate him,
b) failing to provide a functional behavior assessment for behavioral issues,
c) failing to perform a speech and language evaluation and provide services,
d) failing to provide appropriate extended school year services in the summer after fifth grade, and

e) failing to provide an appropriate program and placement for the fourth-
   and fifth-grade school years.

DISTRICT POSITION

At all times, the district stated Josh has been eligible for special education
as a student with an intellectual disability. They also stated he exhibited
behavioral difficulties. The IEP team concluded his behavior impeded his
learning and that of his peers, but the district agreed they did not conduct
a functional behavior assessment, nor create a behavior intervention plan,
because they have found some students with behavioral issues benefit from
"in-school restrictions" and are included as a result of those actions. The
district also clarified Josh was eligible and received ESY services for the
summer after fifth grade.

The district went on to say the IEP created for Josh's fourth- and fifth-grade
years described a course of study of functional academics. Both IEPs included
goals in independence, reading, writing, math, social skills, career skills,
self-advocacy, and receptive and expressive language. The district stated it
developed the goals and objectives of the IEP based on observations from the
teachers, and used anecdotal evidence of his making progress in school and
also anecdotal evidence of his behavioral problems. The district also stated
the teachers worked with him and he did not have difficulty with speech and
language skills, and therefore there was no need for a speech evaluation.

DECISION

The hearing officer, absent a clear IEP-derived standard for determining the
amount of time of compensation for that summer, calculated the compensation based on the amount of time that the parent and district agreed to for that
summer: sixty hours.

ORDER

1. Josh shall receive five hours of compensatory education for each day of
   fourth and fifth grade and until such time as the district conducts appropriate evaluations and develops and implements an appropriate IEP.
2. This compensatory education shall not be used in place of services that
   are contained in any present or future IEPs. The nature of the services

shall be decided by the parent and may include any educational, thera-peutic, developmental, or vocational services that further the goals of the IEP. The services may be used after school, on weekends, or during the summer, and may be used after the student reaches twenty-one years of age. The services may be used hourly or in blocks of hours. The district has the right to challenge the reasonableness of the hourly cost of the services.

3. The student shall receive a speech and language evaluation to determine the necessity and appropriateness of speech and language services.
4. The district shall reimburse the parents for the costs of the independent educational evaluation (IEE) performed by the parents' private evaluator.

JOSH: SPECIAL EDUCATION DIRECTOR RESPONSE

There are several process issues raised by this case.

1. Goals in functional academics—based on observation and anecdotal
2. Behaviors not addressed in IEP
3. No functional behavior assessment (FBA)—district stated behaviors interfered
4. IEP provided speech and language goals—school staff shared student has no speech and language needs
5. No evaluation to determine speech and language needs
6. Appropriate ESY program
7. Compensatory education is appropriate
8. IEP developed off a missing evaluation
9. Paying for the IEE

An IEP must be responsive to all of the needs identified in the evaluation. This student must have had an evaluation at some point to initially qualify for special education services. If the district is not able to locate the evaluation, conducting a new evaluation would be prudent. An evaluation is the baseline data used to create an IEP and measure progress. This not only includes standardized assessments, but must include "evaluations and information provided by the parents of the child; current classroom-based, local, or State assessments, and classroom-based observations; and observations by teach-ers and related service providers; and . . . what additional data, if any, are needed" [§300.305(a)(1), (i)–(iii); (a)(2)]. This baseline data can then be used to develop an appropriate IEP, in which data from the proceeding IEP can be used to create the next IEP.

Districts are also required to conduct a reevaluation "at least once every three years, unless the parent and the [district] agree that a reevaluation is unneccessary" [§300.303(b)(2)]. The facts in this case, as presented, did not address when the previous evaluation was conducted; however, if an evaluation is missing, another should be conducted. The IEP team determines the assessments needed—according to the facts presented, there was conflicting opinion regarding speech and language needs (staff reported that speech and language skills were appropriate, yet goals and services were not provided in that area). If a standardized assessment and more observations had been conducted, the team would have then had the opportunity to develop an informed IEP.

In regard to the claim that the IEP was not "reasonably calculated to confer meaningful educational benefit," and did not provide meaningful benefit for those chosen needs, the district cannot argue that it has provided FAPE. One indicator that supports the parents' claim here is that the goals did not change. If an IEP is reasonably calculated and the services appropriate, there should be progress notes from year to year. The lack of progress (updating of goals) should have been a red flag to the district that some changes needed to take place. FAPE requires a program reasonably calculated to confer meaningful educational benefit for all identified needs and for needs that should have been identified had an appropriate evaluation occurred. In this case, the parents claim that neither a speech and language evaluation, nor a systematic behavioral evaluation (whether FBA or some other assessment) was conducted. Hence, the hearing officer has to determine if the IEP is fundamentally flawed in that it is unresponsive to needs, for which the district provided a general notion as witnessed by the unsubstantiated goals in two areas in the IEP.

When an IEP team determines that a student's behavior is impeding his learning, they are required to address that issue. Therefore, following that determination, the team needed to determine how the student's behaviors were going to be addressed in the IEP. This may have included conducting a functional behavior assessment (FBA) and developing a positive behavior support plan (PBSP) or a behavior plan. The district failed to do that.

If the student's disability includes needs in speech and language, the IEP team has an obligation to conduct an evaluation sufficiently comprehensive to identify all of the child's special education and related service needs. Evaluations identify needs and then these needs drive the development of the IEP. Without an evaluation sufficient to identify all of the student's needs one cannot determine what services should be provided. The district may not substitute the subjective and unsystematic judgment of members of the IEP team for a systematic and thorough evaluation. Given the fact that the IEP team, without a sound basis in evaluation, has determined Josh has needs in the area of speech and language, the district must conduct a systematic and thorough evaluation in this area, even if it rules out the need for additional services.

Specifically, according to the regulations in effect at the time of the District's actions:

> Evaluation means procedures used in accordance with §§300.500 (2) to determine whether a child has a disability and the nature and extent of the special education and related services that the child needs. (34 CFR §300.12)

Furthermore, the regulations in effect at the time of the district's actions and the proposed regulations pursuant to the 2004 reauthorization of IDEA state:

> In evaluating each child with a disability under §§300.531 through 300.536, the evaluation is sufficiently comprehensive to identify all of the child's special education and related services needs, whether or not commonly linked to the disability category in which the child has been classified. [34 CFR §300.532(h)]

Thus, it was the responsibility of the district to determine if a speech and language evaluation was necessary to determine the nature and extent of the special education and related services the child needs.

Given that the IEP was basically the same for both years, and there was no comprehensive evaluation completed, the hearing officer determined that both the evaluation and IEP were flawed and could not have been reasonably calculated to provide meaningful benefit, and concluded that the district denied FAPE. Since the ESY services for the summer after fifth grade should have been based on an appropriate IEP, but the one in existence was flawed and based only on a general conversation between the summer teacher and the regular school year teacher, any benefit was not the result of "reasonable calculation," but chance. Without data to support responsiveness of any claimed benefit to the student's IEP goals, the hearing officer concluded it did not confer meaningful benefit. As such, any benefit derived (and no meaningful measure of benefit, if any, was derived) cannot be said to meet the standard of meaningfulness—meaning addressing all needs. Accordingly, Josh is entitled to compensation for the ESY program for the summer after fifth grade. The dispute in this situation was not based on the number of hours of ESY, but whether the services were appropriate. It is difficult to claim the services were appropriate when the ESY teacher did not review the IEP.

Compensatory education is a remedy designed to provide eligible students with the services they should have received pursuant to a free appropriate public education (FAPE). Thus compensatory education is an in-kind remedy. A child is entitled to compensatory educational services if the child is exceptional and in need of special education and related services (i.e., eligible for FAPE) and if through some action or inaction of the district, the child was denied FAPE. Unlike reimbursement for private schooling or independent evaluations, compensatory education is due the child, not the parent.

Finally, in accordance with §300.502, the district will pay the cost of an independent educational evaluation (IEE). This is a parental right when parents disagree with the school district's finding. Since there are behavioral concerns a behavioral assessment would have been prudent. The same applies for speech and language assessment. Since the parents felt the evaluation was incomplete due to these specific areas, they were able to request an independent educational evaluation. Once a parent requests an IEE, the district can ask them what they disagree about, but cannot force them to respond. The district will then give the family a suggested list of independent evaluators. Once the IEE is completed, the district is under obligation to consider the results of the evaluation, but not necessarily carry out its recommendations.

Documentation is an important part of the special education progress. Districts must have data and assessments to justify programming decisions. Since there was a concern by the parents in regard to the speech and language testing and concerns about the appropriateness of the IEP written, it would have been best to conduct an evaluation so that there was more current data to make programming decisions.

Determining appropriateness of an IEP can be difficult when students have a large number of needs. However, this is why the transition portions are so important. If the team knows the future plans of the student, then the program can be more appropriately focused to help the student be successful in those plans. This requires districts and families to work closely together.

JOSH: DISTRICT ATTORNEY RESPONSE

There were a number of shortcomings that significantly weakened the school district's hand in this case. Although it does not seem to be a main point in the decision, the fact that Josh was receiving special education services about 75 percent of the time in a special education setting and 25 percent of the time in a general education setting seems out of whack. That percentage strikes me as particularly important when Josh did not make much progress. Another weakness in the district's case is the fact that many of the goals in Josh's IEP did not change between his fourth and fifth grade years. At a minimum, this creates the perception that the district fell into the rut of simply carrying over the same goals from the prior year for the sake of expediency. That practice has been a problem for numerous districts and is an example of the kind of practice at play in the Supreme Court's decision in the *Endrew F.* case.

In addition to the appearance of complacency in the development of the IEP, the facts paint a picture of the failure to properly evaluate Josh before adopting a new IEP in his fifth grade year. Despite his speech and language issues, as well as behavioral issues, the failure to evaluate in those areas undermines the integrity of the IEP. Furthermore, even assuming the IEP was done properly, the ESY instructor's failure to review the IEP undermines the argument that FAPE was provided during that period. The disregard for the IEP also supports a narrative that the district was simply going through the motions with Josh's evaluations and IEP development, to the point that the ESY instructor simply ignored the IEP. The narrative is also supported by the fact the IEP developed after fifth grade was based on an evaluation authored by Josh's special education teacher rather than the school psychologist. As if that was not bad enough, the IEP was created before the reevaluation was complete. This set of facts would make it incredibly difficult for the district's attorney to effectively advocate that FAPE was provided and that the IEP was reasonably calculated to provide meaningful benefit for Josh.

Based on the facts of this case, the decision is not surprising due to the missed opportunities to evaluate and miscues on the development of the IEP. However, the award of compensatory education is troubling since the parent get to decide the nature of the services that will be provided to further the goals of the IEP. This is problematic because the essence of this case is that the district failed to properly evaluate and develop an IEP. By making the services provided through compensatory education a parent's menu option, the decision may ultimately result in Josh not receiving the services he needs because the parents' decision might not be based on proper evaluations. While parents usually have a strong sense of what might address their child's needs, their choices will not always hit the mark in helping a student make progress.

JOSH: PARENT ATTORNEY RESPONSE

Josh's case provides an opportunity to share why I believe IEP teams should think of themselves as scientists instead of teachers. While I am cautious when I tell parents that their children should be treated like a science experiment, this change in mindset provides the necessary shift away from an adult's traditional role of teaching children. Instead, this new role focuses on understanding how the child best learns.

As a former teacher, I know how easy it is to fall into the "we teach how we were taught" mindset. Teachers often resist the need to develop a written plan that provides the details of how they plan to do their job. Accommodations like preferential seating and extended time are not spelled out in detail, because teachers believe it is understood how these accommodations will be implemented. A scientist would disagree.

A scientist's job is to gain knowledge. To do so, they use the scientific method, which provides a step-by-step approach to answer questions and learn about a subject. Like the IDEA, the method values objective and observable data. When a hypothesis doesn't pan out, there is a process to make adjustments. The scientist's feelings and subjective views are eliminated from the process. The IEP process should follow a similar framework.

The first three steps of the scientific method align with the steps to arrive at a completed IEP.

1. Ask a question.
2. Do background research
3. Create a hypothesis.

First, the team asks questions and does background research to determine the student's present levels. Evaluation reports are generated, and needs are identified. This information fills out the IEP form to set up the "experiment." By the end of this process, we have a hypothesis that the student will make meaningful educational progress when given the supports and services provided in the IEP.

The remainder of the scientific method outlines the procedures for implementing the IEP. We test our hypothesis by delivering the specially designed instruction (SDI) and accommodations. Periodically, we pause to collect data and report progress. If the procedure is not working, we troubleshoot the procedure and reconvene an IEP meeting. If it is working, we analyze the data and draw conclusions.

If Josh's IEP team viewed themselves as scientists, they would have immediately recognized the holes in their process. The team delivered speech and language instruction without asking any questions, doing background research, or creating a hypothesis. There was no plan other than to provide services and see if they stuck. The same could be said for his summer programming, which was guided by informal discussions. The complete lack of "reasonable calculation" would not pass muster in a scientist's lab, and it shouldn't in a teacher's classroom.

Case Three: Calvin

Behavioral Issues

BACKGROUND

Calvin is a fifth grade student who qualifies for special education and related services under the disability category of Emotional Disturbance and the secondary disability categories of Autism, Other Health Impairment and Speech/Language Impairment. Over the past year he has had a number of behavioral problems in the classroom. The district feels he needs a more restrictive placement in order to receive an appropriate education. The parents feel it is absolutely necessary for him to stay in his local school and not be moved.

Calvin currently participates in regular education classrooms for all of his subjects except for English language arts. He is currently scheduled to be educated in his general education classes for 90 percent of his day. He is pulled out of the general education class only for language arts. The district noted he is diagnosed with ADHD, ASD, and ODD (Attention Deficit Hyperactivity Disorder, Autism Spectrum Disorder, and Oppositional Defiant Disorder, respectively). At school he does not take any medication.

His classroom teachers state he benefits from chunking assignments and extra time to complete tests/quizzes. Typically, his difficulties are with work completion and following classroom/school rules. He excels in the areas of reading fluency.

The district provided Calvin with a 1:1 aide that supported him throughout the day. She helped the teachers implement his positive behavior support plan (PBSP) in the classroom and assisted him with his daily needs. The aide also used various strategies to help Calvin complete his work. The aide was integral to his completing his work. The district stated she was always trying to find reinforcers that helped increase the amount of classwork he completed. She would offer him a menu of reinforcers but most times he would refuse. She facilitated breaks from class and encouraged him to follow classroom and school rules. She would try to encourage him to complete his classwork but did not do the work for him. If he had any incomplete assignments, she would either collect them to work on the next day or send them home if he hadn't completed them within a day or two. The only time she would not assist him was during lunch. He is very attached to the aide but her presence does not eliminate his unexpected behaviors. She is very aware of how he is doing in class and the most important service she provides is getting him out of the classroom before his behaviors escalate. If she is able to get him to de-escalate, she will then slowly get him to do his work, and if it goes well, rejoin class with him.

Calvin has a mental health aide from an outside agency that supports him in school for a maximum of sixteen hours per week. The daily behavior logs indicate that Calvin often feels crowded by the mental health aide, who follows him around in addition to his 1:1 aide. The school aide reported that she would sit away from Calvin in these situations to make him feel less crowded.

The district stated that Calvin's teachers and aides have done the following to ensure his success in the regular education classroom and in the special education classroom:

1. Introduction and lessons using "The Zones of Regulation"
2. Explanation of emotions with use of visual tools from "The Zones of Regulation"
3. Use of a reward system using highly preferred items and a daily tracking chart for rewards earned
4. Positive behavior reinforcement
5. Use of verbal and nonverbal reminders to stay on task
6. Emails home to communicate behaviors of concern
7. Preferential seating within the classroom
8. Visual timer used for classroom tasks
9. 1:1 "pep-talks" to motivate him in the morning
10. Limiting distractions within the classroom environment
11. Avoiding known, possible behavioral triggers when possible
12. Frequent communication with other professionals that work with Calvin to ensure his behavior plan is being implemented
13. Extended time for taking tests in small group setting
14. Use of planned ignoring of small, attention-seeking types of behavior to avoid a larger behavioral issue
15. Providing high-interest items for rewards or use during breaks
16. Agenda sent home daily for communication between school and home
17. Modeling of expected social skills and strategies
18. Repetition of directions to assure understanding

Additionally, the district provided for chunking of assignments into smaller, more manageable pieces; nonverbal reminders to not pick at himself during class; implementation and closely following the behavior-reduction strategies for de-escalation; wait time to respond to directives, questions, and directions to return to task; assisting in de-escalation by removing others from the room to ensure student safety; constant reevaluation of strategies and which to use; use of a calm speaking voice and overall manner in dealing with unexpected behaviors; and giving access to an empty classroom for independent work space when needed to eliminate distractions.

Despite the many accommodations that the district made for Calvin, many of his grades have gone down since the first marking period. There are, however, areas where he has made improvements in his grades. The most helpful service the teacher provided was the chunking of his assignments and extended time on his tests and quizzes. If an assignment seemed too large or overwhelming, he was likely to refuse to complete it. The chunking of assignments helped him complete his classwork. This is similar to when he is given tests. He is often overwhelmed by the whole test and needs more time to work through them. If he is able to do them section by section with less time constraints, he is more likely to put in effort.

During the first half of fifth grade, Calvin has engaged in the following behaviors: biting/sucking/picking his skin or hair on his skin, verbal/nonverbal protests, and mouthing inedible objects (which may result in his eating them). If the behavior escalates, Calvin may also engage in the following behaviors: physical aggression (hitting, kicking), environmental destruction (throwing objects, pushing over furniture, destroying materials), or eloping from the classroom and/or school building. The updated FBA completed by the educational team indicated the perceived functions of the behaviors of concern were to escape instruction/directions given to him. The continuation of the behaviors was perceived to be maintained by attempts to gain attention from adults and peers. During some of the behavioral episodes, Calvin's attention-seeking behavior has escalated to the point that staff must intervene to keep him and others around him safe. He has been pulled out of his fifth-grade classroom eighty-two times in the first half of the school year due to either his screaming, his crawling on the floor, or his kicking of the aide in the shins.

DISTRICT POSITION

The district stated Calvin is a child experiencing the aforementioned disorders and/or disabilities for which the following recommendations are made:

That his IEP be modified or amended to address the results of the evaluation, to include remedial interventions as well as accommodations, compensatory strategies and assistive technologies, and occupational and speech/ language therapies. Calvin would also benefit from cognitive-behavioral interventions addressing his ADHD and executive functioning. Finally, attention training as well as behavioral modification methods or techniques could be implemented.

Due to the severity of his behaviors, the district is seeking to have his education be provided in a more restrictive location until his behaviors improve. The district feels that the behaviors he is engaging in, despite all of the interventions that have been tried, are impeding his learning and that of the students around him.

PARENTS' POSITION

The parents acknowledge he has some behavioral issues. However, they do not believe the district has done enough to provide him supports. They want the fifth-grade teacher to be changed, and stated that many of his behaviors are the result of the other students picking on him in the classroom. They had an independent educational evaluation completed on him and the results from their independent evaluator stated he needs reduced stimulation from the classroom, a male fifth-grade teacher, and a room in the building for him to de-escalate.

The parents also stated that a support group they attended for parents of students with disabilities told them to hold firm and make sure Calvin attends the same school he would go to if he were not disabled. They appreciated the work of the aide; however, they felt the aide was preventing him from making progress in the general education curriculum.

They also pointed out that Calvin does not do well on buses, and if the district is able to move him to a more restrictive location, he would have to ride a bus (or another form of transportation) for thirty minutes each way. The parents also stated that if he went to a different school he would not be able to interact with his school peers in the afternoon or on weekends because they live too far away.

Finally, they wanted the district to do more before the decision was made to move him to a more restrictive placement.

DECISION

The hearing officer ruled that despite the parents not wanting to move their son to a more restrictive placement, the district has made numerous attempts to include the student in the school, and that therefore it is appropriate for the student to be placed in a more restrictive placement.

Specifically, the hearing officer was impressed with:

1. The amount of support provided by a dedicated aide for the student
2. The academic accommodations provided to allow the student to be able to try to master the curriculum
3. The work of the district in the development and implementation of the PBSP
4. 1:1 "pep-talks" to motivate the student in the morning
5. Limiting distractions within the classroom environment
6. Avoiding known, possible behavioral triggers when possible
7. Frequent communication with other professionals that work with Calvin to ensure his behavior plan is being implemented
8. Extended time for taking tests in a small group setting
9. Use of planned ignoring of small, behavior-seeking types of behavior to avoid a larger behavioral issue

The hearing officer went on to state that it is obvious that the decision to move Calvin to a more restrictive placement is one that is not being taken lightly; however, it will allow him to receive more support and allow him to move forward in the curriculum. The hearing officer went on to state that this did not factor into the decision, but at the end of fifth grade Calvin would be moving to a new school anyway and the level of supports at the new school (if he did not go to a more restrictive placement) would likely cause a difficult transition.

CALVIN: SPECIAL EDUCATION ADMINISTRATOR RESPONSE

Process Issues District Needed to Address

This case is really about least restrictive environment (LRE). IDEA requires IEP teams to consider possible placements and choose the one that allows the student to have access to and make progress in the curriculum, but in a setting that is with nondisabled peers to the maximum extent possible. School districts work very hard to make sure this happens. In this particular case, we see what many school districts attempt when trying to adhere to this regulation. The regulation goes on to say that "special classes, separate schooling, or other removal of children with disabilities from the regular educational environment occurs only if the nature or severity of the disability is such that education in regular classes with the use of supplementary aids and services cannot be achieved satisfactorily" [§300.114(a)(2)(ii)]. In cases such as this one, it is up to the team to determine at what point the student is no longer benefiting from and making progress. At that point more restrictive environments are to be explored. This can be difficult when the school and family do not agree on what FAPE for that student entails.

There are a few things to consider here. First, the idea of a "continuum of placements." This term is not used in the actual regulations, but is used in the commentary of the regulations. Essentially what it means is that districts must offer a wide range of "placements" in order to meet student's needs. Placements on a continuum would range from services in the general education classroom with no accommodation, modifications, or special education services to a residential placement away from the student's home school and nondisabled peers. These examples both describe a "location," but a placement could include anything in between, such as all classes being in the general education classroom with some accommodations and modifications, or special education services provided in the classroom by the general education teacher, paraprofessional, or special education teacher. It could also mean the student receives an alternate curriculum in the general education classroom. A student could also receive part of their education in the home school or in a general education classroom and part in a day treatment program. The possibilities are endless and individualized to a student's needs. The intent of this part of the law is to have teams consider any possible option and choose the one that ensures the student is able to have access to and progress in the curriculum with nondisabled peers to the greatest extent possible.

There has been debate about having a 1:1 paraprofessional in the general education classroom with a student with a disability, and if this is more socially restrictive than if the student received their education in a setting with only other disabled peers. There has been some research about the social stigma that comes with having an adult supporting a student all day. Teams needs to seriously consider this stigma. One-on-one paraprofessionals may seem like the answer but there are definite repercussions and they are only one option for consideration. This case demonstrates how the district took the intent of least restrictive environment seriously and did try multiple "placements." However, the discussion for us ends there. This case does not provide enough detail for the reader to pass judgement on the IEP team's decision or if the choice to move to a residential setting would be appropriate. The team should further discuss what services are provided in the more restrictive setting, and whether those services are available in the student's current school.

Moving a student to a more restrictive placement is a decision that should not be taken lightly. However, it can also be an appropriate placement at the time. IEP teams have a great responsibility when making placement decisions and they should not be made easily.

CALVIN: DISTRICT ATTORNEY RESPONSE

The facts in this case raise the issue of whether Calvin's placement outside of his regular school is the least restrictive option. Although parents frequently want their child to remain in the same school, the decision ultimately should be based on whether a different placement is appropriate based on Calvin's identified disabilities. Therefore, the hearing officer is correct in focusing on the efforts of the district to provide support. However, there are some considerations that seem to be lacking in the district's response.

While the district has identified multiple issues, the kinds of behavioral issues Calvin is exhibiting beg the question of whether he requires further evaluation. Additionally, the reaction to the mental health aide should be a cue to the district that maybe the use of that aide or the techniques being employed are not effective. It is not clear whether the supports offered by teachers in the form of chunking assignments and providing extended time on tests are being provided consistently. It is uncertain whether the school personnel who are implementing the supports are on the same page. If the supports are being provided inconsistently, this is going to show up as a weakness in the district's case.

Because IDEA requires Calvin to be placed in the least restrictive environment to the maximum extent possible, I would be concerned whether the district has determined the extent of Calvin's mental and behavioral issues before changing his placement. For example, although Calvin has been on medication for multiple diagnoses, he is not taking medication at school, and there is no further explanation for this. Therefore, the school district should find out whether an accommodation to take the medication might help with the behavioral issues. Additionally, the parents have also expressed concern about Calvin being picked on in the classroom. In addition to contributing to some of Calvin's behaviors, there is nothing in the facts provided that indicates the district has done anything to investigate or deal with that issue. That creates potential exposure for a discrimination claim based on Calvin's disability status.

While the hearing officer's decision may be the right result and the district did a great deal to provide support, it is important to be certain to identify all of the issues impacting the student's educational program. Finally, if there are changes that could have an impact, such as addressing the medication issue or evaluating the use of an outside aide, the district would be well advised to consider those options before changing Calvin's placement.

CALVIN: PARENT ATTORNEY RESPONSE

I hope I would have had the foresight to guide Calvin's parents away from this due process hearing. When parents call our office to fight for their kid to be included in the regular education classroom, our initial reaction is to support the fight. The emotional baggage coupled with the decision to place a child in a more restrictive educational placement is often hard to overcome. However, Calvin's situation highlights several district actions that I hope would have made me pause and consider if the change was the correct move for Calvin.

Calvin's opinion describes an educational program filled with quality data and a highly individualized education program. But it's the district's level of communication that would have scared me away from the claim. First, the district was in constant communication with the family through regular emails and a daily agenda. Second, they welcomed the involvement of outside professionals to ensure the behavior plan was implemented. This signals to me that the district had nothing to hide and was interested in getting it right for Calvin.

We often hear from parents who are told that their Therapeutic Support Staff (TSS) or Behavior Support Curriculum (BSC) service provider is not welcome in the school. Parents request more communication and promises are made but rarely followed through on. This was not the case here. The district was an open book that welcomed outside input and involvement.

They also showed a willingness to change. They responded to his increased needs by a completed and updated FBA (functional behavior assessment). They did not sit back and assume they understood the function of his behavior because they were familiar with him. Educational records that reflect frequent communication and updated plans are rarely given to us by districts. I believe this is a causation of problems, not just a correlation. The more frequently you communicate with parents and attempt to update the educational plan, the less likely the family will contact an attorney.

Case Four: Manuel

Least Restrictive Environment

BACKGROUND

This case involves a student with autism and intellectual disabilities eligible for special education. The parents alleged the student is not included to the maximum extent possible, and that he has been denied appropriate services. They stated his educational program needs to be dramatically changed and he is due extensive compensatory education.

The district argued that they fully implemented the program from a previous district as they saw fit, that he requires a more restrictive placement, and that he is not due compensatory education because at all times he has been provided appropriate services.

Manuel is a seventeen-year-old junior in high school eligible for special education as a student with autism and an intellectual disability. Manuel's measured achievement in academic and adaptive behavior functioning lies in the average, adequate to adaptive, or borderline ranges. Manuel has a full-scale IQ of 67. He also receives occupational therapy and speech and language therapy for pragmatic language. Manuel is independent and his self-help skills are functional. Manuel tends to be hesitant in social situations; he defers to peers in a group for answers, and looks down at the floor rather than engaging in social interaction. Manuel is an independent, compliant young man. He is polite and follows rules. Manuel has generally good health; however, he does have some gastrointestinal problems requiring periodic visits to the nurse. These issues are often accommodated by immediately leaving a situation to go to the restroom. In his previous district, Manuel played on the football team and as a result of an injury, required knee reconstruction surgery. His knee is fine, although he is no longer able to play football.

Prior to coming to the school involved in this complaint, Manuel was in a general education homeroom, ate lunch with his friends, and participated in school activities. He was independent and navigated around the school, going from class to class and participating in extracurricular activities without the assistance of a paraprofessional. He was not only a member of the football team, but also participated in the school's theater program.

Manuel was eligible for occupational therapy in his previous school district. He has not received occupational therapy (OT) in the current district, nor were there any occupational therapy goals in his IEP. He was also receiving supports for assistive technology in the previous district. Specifically, his OT goals were incorporated with the use of assistive technology (AT). The previous districts goals were: Manuel will utilize his word processor in all application classes to complete longer written assignments at an 80 percent accuracy, and Manuel will be independent with utilizing his word processor, sending his work on the word processor to the computer, making corrections on the computer, and printing his papers at an 80 percent success rate.

Manuel has had some behavioral issues. The previous district had a positive behavior support plan addressing specific strategies to help him in social interactions.

PARENTS' POSITION

The parents state that in his previous school Manuel received special education services in which he was included with general education peers in elective classes. Since Manuel moved to the current district he has been assigned full-time to the class for students with intellectual disabilities. He is not permitted to attend regular classes unless accompanied by an aide, and only if other students with intellectual disabilities attend the same elective class. Manuel has to eat at a specific special education table with his teacher and aide in the cafeteria. Manuel's class schedule does not include content area subjects such as social studies, science, English/language arts, and/or health, which are required for Manuel to meet graduation requirements. It is noteworthy that Manuel wants to graduate with his peers. He was under the impression that he would not receive a regular diploma and had to stay in school until he was twenty-one because he is in a class for students with intellectual disabilities. The parents state this is very discouraging to Manuel.

Manuel rides a special education bus. Due to the lateness of bus arrival and students entering the cafeteria late, the special education class misses the first designated period of instruction on a daily basis. Manuel's special education bus leaves twenty minutes earlier than his general education peers'. He often misses end of the school day pep rallies and is not able to participate in after-school activities.

Manuel's class for students with intellectual disabilities is required to participate in adaptive physical education (PE). The parents agree that he has had knee issues in the past due to an injury while playing football at the previous district; however, the only limitation imposed on him as a result of the knee surgery is that he is no longer able to play contact football. Therefore, adaptive PE is not necessary, nor is there a reason in the present levels of his IEP indicating a need for any assistance whatsoever.

There is no behavioral support plan for Manuel in the current district. The current IEP requires him to stand up for himself. The parents are concerned that this would have him placed in a bullying/harassment situation in which he would have to confront others. He is not being taught strategies for how to interact with others.

Finally, the parents allege there are no specific math or reading goals in his current IEP. He is expected to receive special education and related services full-time in a special education classroom; however, there are no specific math or reading goals that provide guidance about his progress in the classroom.

DISTRICT POSITION

The district responds that at all times it has implemented the current IEP for Manuel. The parents agreed to the most recent IEP, and that is what is being implemented, exactly as it was written.

Regarding the specifics of the parents' complaint, it is the policy of the district to provide specialized transportation for all students with intellectual disabilities. There is an aide assigned to the bus to assist the students with their needs. The reason for the bus arriving to school late and leaving early is due to the length of the bus ride and the distance that it is required to cover both before and after school.

The district also provides adaptive PE to all students in the class for students with intellectual disabilities due in part to scheduling, but also because there is a dedicated aide assigned to be a part of the class that can provide assistance when necessary.

The district feels it is necessary to educate Manuel full-time in the special education class due to the level of functioning Manuel demonstrates in reading and math.

Manuel does not receive occupational therapy supports because there has been no evidence in the classroom that he would require occupational therapy. The teacher in his full-time special education class states he sees no need for OT, and that accommodations he might need are easily provided by the teacher or an aide.

The district also states there are no specific math or reading goals for Manuel that will allow the teacher flexibility to work with him on the current skill necessary for him to be successful in his work program, which the district provides as a part of transition. The district states it is proud of the transition program and Manuel is able to spend two hours a day, two times a week in a work setting helping to pack boxes, and that he is learning valuable work skills. The curriculum for the classroom is based on the needs of the worksite. Sometimes there is additional reading or math instruction needed, but it is based on the needs of the worksite at the time.

DECISION

The hearing officer admonished the district for not providing Manuel an education in as least restrictive an environment as possible. The hearing officer ordered an immediate IEP team meeting to address these issues. The hearing officer also awarded 798 hours of compensatory education. This calculation was based on the number of days he has been registered with the district, minus the time he missed for knee surgery (one month).

Calculations were based on the following:

1. Shortened schedule for life skills students when compared to general education peers, due to specialized transportation

   • Compensatory education for no first period of instruction:
   • 20 minutes per day for 315 days (180 for 11th grade + 135 for 10th grade)
   • = 6,300 minutes / 60 minutes
   • = 105 hours

2. No specific math goals for Manuel

   • Compensatory education for math:
   • 40 minutes per day for 315 days (180 days for 11th grade + 135 for 10th grade)
   • = 12,600 minutes / 60 minutes
   • = 210 hours

3. No specific reading goals for Manuel

   • Compensatory education for reading:
   • 40 minutes per day for 315 days (180 days for 11th grade + 135 for 10th grade)

- = 12,600 minutes / 60 minutes
- = 210 hours

4. Occupational therapy/assistive technology (no occupational goals for Mark in his IEP)

- Compensatory education for lack of assistive technology and occupational therapy:
- 40 minutes per day for 315 days (180 days for 11th grade + 135 for 10th grade)
- = 12,600 minutes / 60 minutes
- = 210 hours

5. No positive behavior support plan or functional behavior assessment

- Compensatory education for lack of FBA and PBSP:
- 1 hour per week for 63 weeks (36 weeks in 11th grade + 27 in 10th grade)
- = 63 hours

MANUEL: SPECIAL EDUCATION ADMINISTRATOR RESPONSE

Least Restrictive Environment

When Manuel transferred, the district needed to determine his needs and how they could be met in the new setting. This could require an evaluation and then the development of an IEP. At times this requires an IEP team to reconvene and determine if all of the services are needed in the current setting or if additional services should be added. It appears the district attempted to implement the previous IEP, but within the parameters of what the district currently offered and not based on what was needed for Manuel. It appears the district attempted to fit Manuel into their programs and not individualize for him and his specific needs. Districts have the responsibility to attempt to educate students with disabilities with their peers to the greatest extent possible; the law does not allow for placement decisions to be made based on the needs of the district.

This case demonstrates multiple examples of the district making decisions based on their needs, for example the issues with transportation, attending general education classes without a paraprofessional, and the mandated lunch seating arrangements. The district also attempted to make placement decisions based on the student's special education label and not his individualized needs. It is important to keep in mind that the category a student is placed in or "qualified" under has nothing to do with determining services or placement. This label can be used to guide the team, but when developing an education plan, decisions are required to be determined based on the student's individualized need, not his disability category and not the district's needs.

It also appears the previous district was working toward getting Manuel as much independence as possible. They were teaching him the skills needed to successfully navigate after high school. This intent is aligned with the purpose of special education to "prepare [students] for further education, employment, and independent living" [§300.1 (a)]. Some of these tasks included the behavioral plan, teaching of strategies to interact with others, attending classes independently with peers, and attending appropriate general education programs (e.g., physical education). When IDEA was reauthorized, this intent was added and now schools have the responsibility to consider what the student with a disability would like to be doing after high school. As students move through their high school program IEP teams will need to continue to hone in on the necessary skills needed for the activities students will be engaging in beyond high school. This may mean that FAPE for them will look very different from that of their general education peers.

Diploma

Another area of great concern here is the parents' complaint that Manuel will not have the opportunity to receive a regular diploma. Each state and/or district may have different regulations and policies to guide the team on how and when a student will be eligible for a regular diploma. However, it does not appear the team has discussed the options for Manuel in this area. The IEP team needs to remember they have the ability to allow Manuel to receive credit for a particular class based on his needs. They will individualize the class to meet his needs and therefore can give him credit. Not all students will need to attend school past the time their age-matched peers graduate, even if they have significant needs. Therefore the team would need to use the transition process outlined in the IEP to determine what Manuel's individual needs are based on what his transition goals are, and plan accordingly.

The biggest concern noted in this case is it appears the district may have a great program they are expecting all students of a certain ability level to participate in. However, they are not individualizing for students within that program and are expecting all to participate in this program as it is set. This does not meet the requirements or the spirit of IDEA.

MANUEL: DISTRICT ATTORNEY RESPONSE

The hearing officer's decision in this case is not surprising, based on some blind spots the district seems to have missed. It also illustrates the substantial impact of compensatory education awards when a school district misses warning signs over a prolonged period of time. Several of the district's practices would make it very difficult for an attorney to provide a good defense. If presented with this set of facts, the best a school solicitor can do is attempt to provide damage control by encouraging the district to take significant steps to remedy problems going forward in the hope that those measures will be satisfactory to the parents.

Unfortunately, it appears that the district is discriminating against students with disabilities in multiple ways. First, it is hard to understand how Manuel would be able to navigate between classes, eat lunch with friends, and play football at his previous school, but in his current school must eat at a special education table with his teacher and aide. There is also nothing in the facts provided that indicates why Manuel would be required to ride a special education bus. This kind of segregation from the rest of the student population can only be rationalized if found necessary after an evaluation and implemented through his IEP.

In addition to the stigma of being separated from other students during lunch and transportation, the separate transportation has resulted in him missing instructional time. That would be a red flag for any hearing officer. Within the last several years, legal issues surrounding the importance of attendance for academic success frequently turn up in numerous areas of education law. It is also hard to understand why the district would not evaluate Manuel for occupational therapy services or assistive technology needs since they were provided at his previous district. The bottom line is that the district should have assessed the student's need for occupational therapy services and assistive technology through an evaluation.

If all of the factors discussed above were not enough, basing the transition program curriculum on the worksite need of packing boxes seems incredibly tone deaf. Frankly, the practices in this case almost seem like they should be set in another decade, when children with disabilities were segregated from the rest of the student population. In addition to being out of step with the requirements and intent of IDEA, many educators would find these practices embarrassing. Therefore, these practices make the possibility of a successful outcome for the district close to impossible.

MANUEL: PARENT ATTORNEY RESPONSE

The possibility of inclusion should not be eliminated because of academic concerns. As stated by the Third Circuit Court of Appeals:

The court [and therefore the IEP team] must pay special attention to those unique benefits the child may obtain from integration in a regular classroom which cannot be achieved in a segregated environment, i.e., the development of social and communication skills from interaction with nondisabled peers. See Daniel R.R., 874 F.2d at 1049 ("a child may be able to absorb only a minimal amount of the regular education program, but may benefit enormously from the language models that his nonhandicapped peers provide"); Greer, 950 F.2d at 697 (language and role modeling from association with nondisabled peers are essential benefits of mainstreaming). . . . As IDEA's mainstreaming directive makes clear, Congress understood that a fundamental value of the right to public education for children with disabilities is the right to associate with nondisabled peers.[1]

Manuel had these peer-based benefits of inclusion at his previous school. He was on the football team, ate lunch with his friends, and participated in extracurricular activities without the assistance of a paraprofessional. It must have been quite a shock to Manuel when he was denied the opportunity to do any of these activities at his new school, just because it was their policy.

IEP stands for individualized education program, not insert educational policy. Local educational agencies (LEAs) should not create special education policies to govern how they educate students with special needs with the level of specificity used for Manuel. Policies represent a generalized plan, principle, or guideline that governs how someone behaves. The IDEA provides all of the plans and principles necessary to provide FAPE to children.

Here the LEA let policies dictate Manuel's education. It had a policy that all children with intellectual disabilities received specialized transportation, all participated in the same PE class, and all had their curriculum based on needs identified at a worksite. When an IEP is being populated by district policies instead of the needs of the child, something is wrong.

LEAs should be wary of thinking, "this is how we always do it" or "it worked for all the other children" when carrying out an IEP. Parents only know what works for their children. They are unlikely to be pacified by district policies.

---

1. *Oberti by Oberti v. Bd. of Educ. of Borough of Clementon Sch. Dist.*, 995 F.2d 1204, 1216–17 (3d Cir. 1993).

Case Five: Sawyer

Assistive Technology

BACKGROUND

Sawyer is a ten-year-old boy with intellectual disabilities who is eligible for special education services. His family moved from a different state to the current district almost exactly one year ago. He has been enrolled in the district ever since. Sawyer has Down syndrome and has a full-scale IQ of 52. His standard scores on adaptive skills behavior measures range from 63 to 73. He is nonverbal, and in the previous district used a voice output system for the iPad, Proloquo. In the previous district he also received behavioral modifications and adaptations in the areas of attention, compliance, and social interactions. His educational program in the previous district during his third-grade school year consisted of 70 percent special education in a classroom for students with intellectual disabilities, while he was included with grade-level peers for 30 percent of his day. He participated in general education for art, music, physical education, homeroom, lunch, recess, and extracurricular activities.

Sawyer was reported as having good health, his relationships with adults are characterized as good, and his relationships with peers are characterized as fair.

Sawyer started school in the present district at the beginning of fourth grade. An IEP was developed at the end of September. The IEP developed and implemented in present district was different from his previous IEP in several areas.

PARENTS' POSITION

The parents state that the new IEP was structurally deficient and that due to the glaring omissions, he was denied a free appropriate public education and therefore compensatory education. The parents are also requesting a new program and placement for his fifth-grade year.

Specifically, the parents have six complaints:

1. Assistive Technology

   The parents state there was no assistive technology in the fourth-grade IEP. Sawyer is nonverbal; the use of assistive technology (a verbal output device) was being used to help Sawyer to communicate his needs and understanding of his environment. His previous district provided him the use of an iPad loaded with Proloquo, and also provided him support three times a week from a speech-language pathologist to assist him in understanding and using the device. There was also training not only for the teachers in the school, but also for the parents on the use of the device.

2. Behavioral Accommodations

   The parents state there were no behavioral accommodations in the fourth-grade IEP. The IEP from the previous district had several accommodations to assist him in working with other students, and ways of helping him to deal with frustration. Although Sawyer is reported as having good adult relationships, it is identified that Sawyer has problems with attention, compliance, and social interactions.

3. Reading Goals

   In his previous district, specific IEP goals were listed that provided Sawyer with functional academic skills in emerging reading skills. For the fourth-grade IEP generated by the district, there were no functional reading goals. Even if the goals were appropriate, there was no progress monitoring to determine effectiveness.

4. Math Goals

   In his previous district, specific IEP goals were listed that provided Sawyer with functional academic skills in emerging math skills. For the fourth-grade IEP generated by the district, there were no functional math goals. Even if the goals were appropriate, there was no progress monitoring to determine effectiveness.

5. Social Studies Goals

   In his previous district, IEP goals in social studies were based on learning functional living skills, community awareness, and so on. For the fourth-grade IEP generated by the district, there were no functional social studies goals. Even if the goals were appropriate, there was no progress monitoring to determine effectiveness.

6. Science Goals

Differing from the other academic subjects, the science goals are exactly the same in third grade as they were in fourth grade. Even if the goals were appropriate, there was no progress monitoring to determine effectiveness.

The reason the parents filed a due process hearing was not so much because of the above complaints, but because of other incidents that happened during the course of his fourth-grade year.

In December of fourth grade, Sawyer was working on a puzzle in the classroom. It was time for lunch and Sawyer was having a problem transitioning from the puzzle activity to lunch. When Sawyer did not follow instructions to go to the lunchroom with his classmates, the teacher called the principal for help. The parents state that the principal, aide, and teacher physically picked up Sawyer and dragged and pulled him to the lunchroom. This caused Sawyer to be upset, cry, and resist being removed. After physically escorting, pushing, and dragging Sawyer through the halls and into and out of the elevator to the cafeteria, the principal physically dropped Sawyer off at the doorway to the cafeteria and left him there, crying uncontrollably. Sawyer was taken to the nurse's room, where his mother came to pick him up.

The parents allege this incident caused trauma for Sawyer resulting in regression. Sawyer immediately began having soiling incidents and night terrors. From that day on, he would not sleep in his own bed. He wanted to be with his parents. He would wake from sleep crying. He continued having toileting accidents.

The parents took Sawyer to a psychiatric institute for a mental health evaluation to help explain why Sawyer was back to not being toilet trained and having night terrors. Sawyer was identified with adjustment disorder with anxiety. Sawyer remained out of school for a few weeks. The parents state that there was never a meeting to discuss the incidents in the hall.

When Sawyer returned to school, the district secured a 1:1 aide for him. Her name was Ms. Emma. Ms. Emma interacted very well with Sawyer. According the parents, Ms. Emma was encouraged by the director of special education and his fourth-grade special education teacher to email or text the parents to assure them that Sawyer was feeling safe in school. The parents were working with Sawyer to comfort him at home and assure him he was going to be safe at school. Ms. Emma was there to help him. Sawyer responded well to her. Toileting issues and night terrors were occurring less frequently. After Ms. Emma's involvement, the last eight weeks of school were rather uneventful.

Sawyer then began his fifth-grade year. The classroom and teacher were new to Sawyer. Ms. Emma returned to the classroom as Sawyer's aide. It appeared that Sawyer was doing well. He was having good days at school, despite the changes in the classroom and teacher. Ms. Emma was a consistent and comforting part of Sawyer's educational program. On or about September 21, the parents were informed that the aide, Ms. Emma, was being terminated. Sawyer was told that Ms. Emma was not going to be there anymore, she was going away. Sawyer came home and told his parents "Sawyer bad, Ms. Emma go." At that point, once again, Sawyer started to have night terrors and toileting accidents. The parents tried to comfort Sawyer and did send Sawyer to school. However, Sawyer was demonstrating a resistance to going to school, something that had not occurred since the restraint that occurred the previous school year.

The parents attempted to find out what happened to Ms. Emma. School administrators said that Ms. Emma was terminated for insubordination. The parents allege that Ms. Emma was terminated for communicating Sawyer's progress to the parents. The parents were surprised as their communication was the same as the previous year. The parents asked to observe in the school to learn if other issues were bothering Sawyer. The parents have not been able to observe Sawyer in the classroom. Sawyer's behaviors at home have deteriorated. The parents returned to the same psychiatric institute they previously visited. Sawyer has been diagnosed, again, with adjustment disorder with anxiety. The parents have asked the school for homebound instruction until Sawyer feels safe.

The parents state these incidents, which have had a negative impact on Sawyer, would not have occurred had a positive behavior support plan or accommodations for his behavioral issues been developed and implemented. In addition, because of Sawyer's inability to verbalize how he is feeling, the abandoned vocal output assistive device has limited Sawyer's communication progress.

They are seeking immediate reinstatement of Ms. Emma as Sawyer's aide in addition to compensatory education for lack of appropriate programming for the fifth-grade year.

DISTRICT POSITION

The district feels the programming and placement for Sawyer is appropriate. He requires intensive services throughout his day and that is what is being provided. He does receive the majority of his education in a class for students with intellectual disabilities. There is one teacher, five students, and two aides directly assigned to the class. Sawyer is also provided a 1:1 aide to assist him with whatever is necessary throughout the day.

The district states that it is clear the parents liked the program from the previous district; however, based on observations, changes were made to the programming he was provided. The district specifically states that its IEP goals in the areas of reading, math, social studies, and science were appropriate and that Sawyer was making progress in the curriculum.

They offered the following as an example of a math goal for Sawyer:

Sawyer will be able to identify and give the value for all coins up to a quarter and the value of coins up to and including a dollar, perform addition and subtraction operations, using manipulatives as needed, and count from 1 to 50 with 100 percent accuracy.

a. Identify penny, nickel, dime, quarter, and dollar bill with 10 percent accuracy on three trials.
b. Comprehend value of coins and dollar bill with 100 percent accuracy on three trials.
c. Solve addition and subtraction problems using manipulatives with 85 percent accuracy on three trials.
d. Complete a hundreds chart from 1 to 50 with 100 percent accuracy on three consecutive trials.

They offered the following as a science goal for Sawyer:

Sawyer will demonstrate his science skills by selecting an appropriate measuring tool for a science or cooking activity and measuring correctly with teacher assistance, with no more than one verbal prompt and with 80 percent accuracy.

a. Given three difference-measuring tools, Sawyer will select the appropriate measuring tool used to measure an amount of a substance with no more than one physical prompt with 70 percent accuracy.

The district offered the following as a social studies goal for Sawyer:

Sawyer will demonstrate his social studies skills by learning his address, including his number and street address, city, and zip code with 100 percent accuracy on three consecutive trials.

The district feels that at all times it provided Sawyer with a free appropriate public education in the areas of math, reading, science, and social studies.

Aide

The district stated that decisions about who is assigned to classes as teachers and aides are the at sole discretion of the district. They stated that parents can request specific individuals as the providers of services, but the district is not obligated to fulfill those requests. Additionally, they are under no obligation to explain to the parents the results of personnel decisions regarding an employee termination or removal.

The district stated that the new aide is well trained and can meet Sawyer's needs.

Restraint

The district stated that it was necessary to remove Sawyer from his location in the hall and he was potentially dangerous to himself and others. The district responded to the parents' allegations by stating that they never picked up Sawyer, nor did they drag Sawyer down the hall. They also stated there was no way the psychiatrist could come to a conclusion that Sawyer was having problems directly as a result of the incident in which he was guided down the hall. They also stated there is no way the psychiatrist could make the claim that Sawyer was having problems directly resulting from the removal of Ms. Emma as his personal aide.

DECISION

The hearing officer ruled in part for the parents and in part for the district.

In ruling for the parents, the hearing officer awarded compensatory education for a lack of assistive technology for the fourth-grade school year. There were no goals established, and it was ordered that Sawyer be provided assistive technology two hours a day for the entire year.

Second, despite not being sought by the parents, the hearing officer ruled that an independent educational evaluation should be completed on Sawyer to help identify present levels and develop appropriate goals.

Third, the district was ordered to develop and implement a positive behavior support plan to teach Sawyer how to transition from activity to activity, comply with instructions, and pay attention to the task at hand.

Fourth, the district was ordered to obtain an assistive technology consult with professionals who understand Sawyer's needs and can properly develop a communication system for him for implementation in the school setting.

In ruling for the district, the hearing officer ruled that the district has the authority to hire and place in classrooms individuals they feel are qualified, and are not required to immediately reinstate Ms. Emma.

The district is not responsible for compensatory education for the fourth-grade year in the areas of reading, math, social studies, or science.

SAWYER: SPECIAL EDUCATION
ADMINISTRATOR RESPONSE

One of the most important things in working with students with disabilities is the relationship with the families. Relationships with families are key in developing and implementing successful programs for students. Based on the information presented, it sounds as though the school and the family needed to have more frequent communication from the beginning. It would have been interesting to understand the data and observations the district used to make the determination that Sawyer no longer required an assistive technology device or a behavioral plan. In this case there was no information presented as to why those major components were dropped. It is interesting in this case that once Sawyer had the significant issue that required him to be "escorted," the IEP team did not reconvene to discuss if a behavioral plan was needed, especially since the district had information from the previous district indicating Sawyer required behavioral intervention. The hearing officer did not address this area; however, it would be prudent for the district to conduct a functional behavior assessment. This will help the district determine the "function" or purpose of the behaviors.

As appears to be the case here, families become very frustrated in making a formal complaint, because it becomes more about procedural issues than the source of the conflict. For example, this family was very frustrated with the termination of Ms. Emma and because of the procedural errors the district made; the family had a stronger case. The district has the obligation to provide progress reports and failed to do so. Another interesting fact that was mentioned in this case that will often get districts in a difficult spot is having a paraprofessional be in charge of communication with a family. Paraprofessionals are an integral part of the education system and imperative to the success of many students. However, the training and understanding of confidentiality and special education regulations provided in FERPA and IDEA are needed to perform this task. Often our paraprofessional staff has a basic understanding, but not the depth needed to appropriately be the sole communicator on a student's performance. Case managers need to be very careful in how and what part of communication they delegate to the paraprofessional. A journal in which the teachers write is often a good tool to use to communicate information to the family. The paraprofessional could be tasked with making sure this gets completed and sent back and forth between home and school, but having the paraprofessional be in charge of the daily communication may be questionable.

SAWYER: DISTRICT ATTORNEY RESPONSE

The outcome of the hearing officer's decision is interesting because it does not specifically address the allegation that the principal's mishandling of Sawyer to get him to go to the cafeteria caused Sawyer to regress. The outcome regarding assistive technology and the specific need for the assistive technology consult seem like predictable outcomes. Although Sawyer's current district is not required to provide supports that are identical, the fact his prior district provided an iPad and speech pathology support should have cued the district for the need to assess in those areas. Other red flags include the lack of progress monitoring in the some of the IEP goals and the fact that the science goals were identical for two years.

Despite a mixed outcome from the hearing officer, there is a high level of potential exposure for the district for a discrimination claim based on allegations related to the principal and the possibility that proper procedures were not followed regarding how Sawyer was physically handled. It is important for districts to remember that simply prevailing on issues involving FAPE does not eliminate the possibility of a different kind of claim under state or federal law. The Office of Civil Rights (OCR) has increasingly warned public schools over the last several years about discriminatory conduct that is directed at students with disabilities. Additionally, in some federal circuits like the Third Circuit, a scenario like this might prompt the filing of a "state-created danger" claim for the deprivation of a student's bodily integrity under the Fourteenth Amendment.

As for the district's handling of the terminated aide, it is true that districts have wide latitude in terms of personnel decisions and must be careful about a former employee's confidentiality. As a public-school employee, the aide has employment rights and there is a system for asserting those rights. Having said that, while the district is not in a position to provide details about the aide's termination, some effort to communicate with the parents about the aide might be warranted. Unfortunately, despite the outcome, it is predictable that there will continue to be legal issues going forward due to the manner in which the district dealt with the allegations of mishandling Sawyer and his regression. Finally, the district's lack of evaluation regarding the regression issues represents another missed cue for the district's identification of possible issues going forward.

SAWYER: PARENT ATTORNEY RESPONSE

Parents frequently seek out an attorney because they are concerned about a single allegation. In special education, the allegations likely stem from discipline or restraint-related actions. Parents view these actions as critical enough to seek legal help. An LEA's reaction to the same event rarely matches the parents' level of concern. While all LEAs must aim to eliminate the use of restraint and unwarranted discipline, an LEA's response to parents may help avoid litigation.

Crisis management 101 dictates that an LEA should handle these incidents by taking responsibility, and being proactive, transparent, and accountable. Conveniently, the IDEA typically requires LEAs to hold meetings with parents after a serious incident occurs. At these meetings, LEAs often fail to give parents the impression that they understand their concerns. Too often the meetings end by the parties agreeing to disagree with the LEA, and the district guards as many facts as possible.

In a crisis, parents feel angry, frightened, and helpless. IEP team members need to acknowledge these feelings and sympathize. I recently represented a student who was ending the school year on homebound instruction because of suicidal concerns stemming from peer bullying and sexual harassment. After the mother shared her concerns for her daughter, the assistant superintendent spoke in a monotone voice and spouted off district policies for the next five minutes. The administrator sounded like a politician who refuses to answer questions. She was completely removed from the parents' concerns. The parents left with no confidence that the district had any better understanding of their child. This is not a positive result for either party.

Even if an LEA acted appropriately regarding the allegation, these inciting incidents rarely lead to a narrowly focused due process complaint. As an attorney, I have an obligation to review a student's records for every potential claim. A careful review of multiple years of educational records often yields numerous claims. These "additional claims" frequently become the central focus of the litigation, rather than the initial incident that caused the phone call. Here, Sawyer's parents sought out legal assistance because of an alleged restraint. Yet they prevailed on claims focused on assistive technology, behavior intervention, and educational evaluations.

LEAs should use these single incidents to perform a more complete check of a child's status. Once the initial crisis is managed, the team should examine any potential areas to improve the delivery of FAPE. While a team may not be able to correct past claims, they can prevent future claims from arising.

Case Six: Caleb

Identification and Changing Schools

BACKGROUND

Caleb's parents moved into the district about halfway through the school year. Their son previously attended a private school for students with behavioral disabilities in another district. The parents are alleging he did not make progress during his time in the school, and therefore is due compensatory education. For the purposes of this case, the two different districts will be referred to as District One and District Two. District One is the original district the student attended, and District Two is the new, receiving district, the one involved in the present dispute.

Caleb is a seven-year-old student eligible for special education and related services as a student receiving services under the disability category of emotional disturbance and, secondarily, a learning disability. During kindergarten, his previous district (District One) evaluated him, wrote an IEP, and eventually placed him at a day treatment facility for students with emotional disturbance. He was placed there due to the severity of his behaviors, specifically aggression toward peers and staff. The school where Caleb was placed was not in the geographical boundaries of District One. District One continued to place him there at the beginning of first grade.

About a third of the way through first grade, Caleb's parents moved to District Two (the District involved in the current dispute), which happened to have within its geographical boundaries the private school he was attending. The parents notified District Two of the move, transferred all records from District One, and told District Two that their son was receiving special education and related services at the day treatment facility.

District Two gathered all the files from the previous district, and seeing there was an IEP with a placement in the day treatment facility, notified the

47

facility they were the new district of record. District Two reviewed the IEP and the previous evaluation report and told the parents that they would be following the directives of the previous IEP and have Caleb continue to receive services at the day treatment facility.

Over the next six months, Caleb did not make progress. His behavioral outbursts appeared to get worse, and his academic performance stagnated. With about a month left in the school year, the parents moved back to District One. Caleb was only a resident of the district involved in this dispute (District Two) for eighty school days.

PARENTS' POSITION

The parents complaint states that Caleb is due compensatory education for the amount of time he was a resident of District Two (eighty school days). They are demanding 6.5 hours a day of compensatory education for a total request of 520 hours. They state the IEP implemented by District Two was inadequate and inappropriate for Caleb, and the fact he regressed during the year also demonstrates the failings of the program. They state District Two should have completed testing on Caleb, and then developed a new IEP during the course of his residence in the district.

The parents claim the evaluation report sent to District Two was more of a speech/language evaluation, and did not address the behavioral needs of Caleb.

Specifically, the parents stated the following about the IEP:

1. The IEP included dreadfully inadequate present levels of education and functional performance that failed to sufficiently describe Caleb's complete educational needs.
2. The IEP included vague goals that failed to include baselines and failed to address Caleb's complete educational needs.
3. The IEP included vague methods for measuring progress.
4. The IEP included drastically inadequate related services that failed to sufficiently address Caleb's complete educational needs.
5. The IEP failed to include a positive behavior support plan that was based on upon a comprehensive functional behavior assessment.

DISTRICT POSITION

District Two responded by stating that at all times it was in full compliance with the law, implementing the IEP at the day treatment facility. They fully paid for the costs of the day treatment facility during the entirety of Caleb's residence in the district, and when the parents moved, they immediately forwarded all information to the new district of residence.

District Two also responded by stating they met with the staff of the day treatment facility several times to ensure the IEP was being implemented as it was written, and received written and verbal assurances that it was being faithfully implemented. District Two was aware he was not making progress related to his behavior, and was in the process of arranging a meeting to develop a new IEP and to discuss the possibility of a new placement.

Additionally, District Two stated it did not commence an evaluation of Caleb when he was registered with them because they viewed him as medically fragile and felt that any evaluation at that time would not yield results that would be helpful in developing a program or placement. They also stated the parents agreed with the IEP that was developed from District One, and they had received IEPs from District One before. The district stated that there were not previous problems with the IEP and they did not expect problems with this one.

District Two again stated it fully implemented the sending district's IEP, and complied with the law by continuing Caleb's placement at the day treatment facility.

Finally, they stated that if they were obligated to provide compensatory education, the amount should be reduced and should not be a full day for each day he was enrolled in District Two, to allow an opportunity for them to revise and rewrite an IEP.

DECISION

The hearing officer ruled in response to all the points raised.

First, the IEP from District One was rightly characterized by the parents as inadequate and inappropriate for Caleb. Specifically, the hearing officer wrote the IEP lacks clarity, is not measurable, and does not relate to the present levels of the IEP, which are very basic and do not provide enough detail to make an informed decision about services he might require. District Two stipulated they fully implemented the IEP that was provided to them by District One. However, the IEP that was implemented, as noted, was very poorly written.

Second, the hearing officer stated that since the IEP implemented while Caleb was a resident of District Two was poorly crafted and inappropriate, he was due compensatory education for the amount of time requested by the parents. Specifically, the hearing officer awarded eighty days of compensatory education, but instead of awarding 6.5 hours a day, he awarded 4.5 hours a day, reducing the amount because of lunch, extracurricular courses (art, music, physical education), and recess. The total amount awarded to the parents was for 360 hours.

Third, the hearing officer dismissed the claims made by District Two that the number of days should be reduced to allow time to redo and develop an IEP that meets Caleb's needs. The hearing officer stated that at no time did District Two initiate an evaluation, take independent data on his progress in the school, or present a draft IEP to the parents. District Two was in the process of developing a draft IEP but had not scheduled a meeting, and this was after Caleb had been a resident of the District for eighty school days (a little over four months).

CALEB: SPECIAL EDUCATION ADMINISTRATOR RESPONSE

There are times when a district determines they are not able to provide FAPE for a particular student. At that point the district will look for a placement that is able to meet the student's needs. Even when the student is placed outside of the district, the student remains a student of that district and the FAPE obligation remains with the school. The FAPE obligation will fall to the district that receives the federal IDEA funds. The district may pay another district or facility to use those funds, but the responsibility remains with the district.

When a student transfers to another district, the IEP team from the previous district needs to determine if the services are appropriate. Because the district remains responsible for FAPE, they need to be aware of how a student is doing when he or she is placed in an alternate setting, and just like if the student were in the district, the school team would need to reconvene to make any changes to a student's program if and when there are areas of concern. Since District Two accepted the placement and IEP of the student, they are responsible for the services that are provided there, in that they must ensure those services continue to be appropriate and the student continues to make progress. The responsibility of FAPE goes well beyond paying for a placement.

Districts need to be very careful when accepting another district's IEP. Often the paperwork will look different and the receiving district can miss a detail of the student's program that will greatly impact the student. It is also important to note that when a district accepts another district's IEP, they are accepting any inadequacies it may have.

Too often, it is easier to assume that an outside agency that has been providing services is giving the student what they need.

CALEB: DISTRICT ATTORNEY RESPONSE

This case reminds me of an important general principle that I frequently mention to educators and administrators. The first principle is to pay attention to the district's status as the LEA (local educational agency) when a student is a resident of the school district. Put another way, once a child is a resident of the district, that district has the obligation to provide FAPE, regardless of what a previous district implemented. This is frequently important in cases involving students receiving instruction in a private school or other private facility. The principle may seem obvious, but all too often districts can lose sight of their responsibility for the evaluation and subsequent implementation of a legally sufficient IEP.

Caleb's situation represents a fact pattern where a student's needs might not come to the attention of a school district like District Two before it is too late. Because the student transferred from a previous district and was attending a private school, there is a good chance the student was not in the forefront of the district's monitoring. That missed cue probably accounts for what could have been a much less costly result for District Two. The shortcoming in District Two's response was the failure to evaluate and implement a more current IEP for Caleb. The fact that Caleb had previous issues related to his emotional disturbance and Caleb's parents placed him in a private school while he was in District One should have prompted a new evaluation. Additionally, without conducting an evaluation of Caleb, how could District Two be assured that Caleb was placed correctly or was receiving the services required for FAPE?

On the other hand, District Two did conduct regular follow-ups with the day treatment facility. However, those follow-ups should have been paired with more contact with the parents to find out their opinion as to whether the current placement under the old IEP was working. Given the fact that District Two had decided to follow District One's IEP, at a minimum there should have been some assessment regarding whether the placement was working. Another curious thing about District Two's willingness to accept District One's placement relates to the cost of the placement. While the decision regarding District Two's placement of Caleb needed to be based on whether placement and IEP were appropriate, a different placement may have been less expensive. District Two will never know that since they took District's One's set of decisions at face value.

The district's response in this case is a reminder that fully paying for the cost of a facility will not carry the day if a hearing officer determines that an IEP is inadequate. District Two left itself open in this case by failing to conduct an evaluation or make changes to the IEP. The reason for not evaluating due to Caleb's medically fragile state does not make a great deal of sense.

The medical issues should raise the question as to whether additional services or accommodations might be warranted. Finally, District Two would have been in a much stronger position to defend this case if it evaluated Caleb and developed a new IEP earlier in the process.

CALEB: PARENT ATTORNEY RESPONSE

It is tempting for an LEA to accept what is given to them by another LEA. In this case, it was the middle of the school year, the private placement was not changing, and the parents had yet to raise any concerns. As a fellow school employee, a level of trust is present in what your fellow teachers are doing. It must have seemed logical to maintain the status quo. Unfortunately, this decision continued a bad IEP and resulted in a costly eighty days of education for the district.

District Two never took full ownership of the bad IEP. They paid the bills and made sure it was being implemented but never fully examined its effectiveness. The IDEA and its regulations demand more. Under 34 C.F.R. §300.323 (e), an LEA team must provide FAPE to the child until they adopt the child's IEP from the previous LEA or develop, adopt, and implement a new IEP. If the family moves to another state, the eligibility requirements may also change. Therefore, if necessary the new state LEA may request an evaluation and develop a new IEP.

I imagine many school employees view the decision as unfair. The LEA had little time to get to know the child and his parents didn't complain. However, the regulations appropriately place the FAPE responsibility with the then-current LEA. No other LEA can make changes to improve the child's IEP. They also give the new LEA the opportunity to fix the mistakes of the previous LEA. There is no requirement that the same IEP remain in effect. The regulations implore the receiving LEA to take ownership of the student and make sure FAPE is being delivered. If it is not, they face liability.

An identified student's enrollment in a new LEA is an important event when I review records for potential clients. It is a time when an LEA is forced to make a decision. These moments of forced decision-making are some of the easiest to evaluate for potential claims. It is fairly simple to determine what the LEA knew or should have known at the time. It is also easier to evaluate the effectiveness of the decision and whether the LEA revisited it at appropriate times. While an LEA should always be mindful of their obligation to provide FAPE, decision points created by the IDEA deserve closer attention.

Here, as pointed out by the hearing officer, District Two did little to ensure the delivery of FAPE. No evaluation was conducted, no independent data collected, and no draft IEP presented. Simply paying the bills and checking on implementation does not suffice.

Case Seven: Bryson

IEP Implementation

BACKGROUND

Bryson is a twelve-year-old male student in the sixth grade. He is identified as eligible for special education as a student with a specific learning disability. He also receives speech and language services. He was identified as eligible for special education in first grade, receiving at first speech and language services and then, later the same year, services as a student with a learning disability.

It is well known that he struggles with his communication skills. Also, during the past year, Bryson has been having problems with coping and social skills. Bryson does not always control his anger and frustration in an appropriate manner. Additionally, he does not always interact with others in an age-appropriate way.

Bryson received special education for his language arts difficulties in fourth and fifth grade for about 100–120 minutes a day. In sixth grade, Bryson was receiving special education for 50 minutes a day.

The precipitating incident that brought about the issues that need to be addressed occurred during a social studies class when Bryson was asked to read by the substitute teacher; Bryson picked up his desk and threw it in the direction of the teacher. No one was hurt, but the other students in the class were clearly upset (as was Bryson). This was not the first time that Bryson had thrown something at a teacher in the past three weeks. The district wanted to have a meeting to discuss having Bryson attend a different school and potentially be assigned to a classroom for students identified as having an emotional disturbance.

The parents did not agree to the request for a change of placement, as the new school the district recommended was located at least an hour away and

the parents did not like the reputation of the school. The district felt it was
necessary for Bryson to go to the special school. The parents disagreed, and
filed a due process hearing.

PARENTS' POSITION

The parents' complaint alleges three things:

1. The district illegally reduced the amount of time Bryson was receiving
   special education and related services from fifth grade to sixth grade. The
   parents allege the decision about programming for Bryson was based on
   administrative convenience, and not on his needs. They state that there
   was no formal plan for reducing the amount of services provided, and
   that he is due back services as a result. During fifth grade he received
   two hours a day of services for language arts. In sixth grade, he received
   services for forty-eight minutes a day.
2. The parents allege the district did not provide Bryson a free appropriate
   public education because Bryson has not made progress on his goals and
   objectives in language arts. The parents obtained an IEE (see below) that
   indicated Bryson was significantly delayed in reading and yet the district
   reduced the amount of services Bryson was provided.
3. The behavior problems Bryson demonstrated in school were the direct result of the inappropriate programming provided by the district. Basically,
   Bryson reads at a first-grade level though he is in sixth grade. He cannot
   read the material, cannot write the material, and needs special education
   beyond his reading class, and he also needs accommodations in his other
   academic subjects as well.

Due to his behavioral issues in sixth grade, Bryson's parents obtained an
independent educational evaluation.

Bryson's WISC-V (Wechsler Intelligence Scale for Children, Fifth Edition) results are included below:

Verbal Comprehension	100
Visual Spatial	94
Fluid Reasoning	100
Working Memory	79
Processing Speed Index	89
Full-Scale IQ	91

The independent educational evaluator also administered the WIAT-III (Wechsler Individual Achievement Test III). Bryson's scores are listed below:

Subtest	Standard Score
Total Reading	51
Basic Reading	49
Reading Comprehension and Fluency	53
Written Expression	51
Mathematics	85
Math Fluency	86

The low scores are also notable because given his reading problems, he was assessed using a third-grade reading passage. In summary, Bryson performed in the Very Low or Low range on all subtests of reading. This suggests Bryson demonstrates very weak abilities in reading comprehension, word recognition, and reading, decoding, and fluency skills when compared to the abilities of his peers. This is an area of significant weakness for Bryson.

He was also administered the Behavior Assessment System for Children–Third Edition (BASC-3). The following items of concern were marked as "Almost Always" occurring: has reading problems; performs poorly on school assignments; has trouble keeping up in class; argues when denied his own way; is easily stressed; is unclear when presenting ideas; overreacts to stressful situations; annoys others on purpose; has a short attention span; and has trouble making friends.

The independent evaluator had teachers provide input regarding Bryson's progress in his sixth-grade curriculum. Notes from the teachers include:

1. Bryson needs to be placed in a class for students with emotional disturbance. Based on past experiences in elementary school, and his outburst this year, this program would benefit Bryson. I also feel Bryson needs to receive some intensive instruction in reading. We are doing him a disservice by passing him to each new grade without being able to read or write at all.
2. I think Bryson is not well suited for the regular education curriculum. I believe that a class for students with intellectual disabilities would help Bryson to be prepared for life beyond school.
3. Bryson displays anger within the classroom. He also has difficulty with attention/focus, participation, accuracy of work, retention of material, preparation for class, task completion, comprehension, homework completion, cooperative behavior, organizational skills, neatness of work, and test/quiz preparation.

4. Bryson is a strong student in the area of math—when it comes to just using numbers. He really struggles when it comes to reading or writing anything. This makes it extremely difficult for him, unless there is someone sitting right beside him one-on-one for any kind of reading or writing activities in school. He seems to be able to comprehend material that is read to him, however. He is also a student who tends to get frustrated easily. If something does not go his way, he tends to either shut down or make a scene in front of the whole class. When he does not complete his work and gets reprimanded for it, he will also argue with teachers and huff and puff.
5. When Bryson is having a good day, he tries very hard to keep it that way. He feels very proud of himself when he achieves any level of success. He is also easily frustrated because he is so far below the level of the rest of the class. He often has major outbursts and meltdowns that require removal from the classroom.

DISTRICT POSITION

The district responded that at all times it has fully implemented the agreed upon IEP. The parents have agreed to all of the IEPs, were fully involved in their development, and provided input on the program and all the evaluations.

The district stated that during elementary school Bryson did receive more time in special education. Now that he is in middle school, the specific requirements of the curriculum prevent his being educated at the same level as when he was in elementary school. He is provided intensive instruction by a certified teacher, but the schedule prevents additional services, unless he goes to a school just for students with learning disabilities.

The district stated that the current program is good for him, because he is included with his nondisabled peers to the maximum extent possible. He has science, social studies, art, PE, music, and math with his peers. He is not singled out for supports because he is considered a part of the regular classroom, which is what schools strive to do for all students eligible for special education.

The district acknowledged he has not made much progress in language arts, but that is why they feel he continues to need special education.

The district did acknowledge the results from the IEE are similar to the results they have seen, and they verified that the comments attributed to the teachers, were, in fact, made by the teachers.

Finally, the district proposed that they complete a functional behavior assessment to help determine if there are specific problems that can be addressed. They did indicate he did not have behavior problems in fifth grade.

THE HEARING

As a part of pre-hearing discussions, the hearing was limited to the following issues:

1. Bryson's program and placement for seventh grade
2. Whether Bryson is due compensatory education for a denial of services

DECISION

The hearing officer ruled on two specific components of the hearing.

First, the hearing officer stated that Bryson complete a different program for his seventh-grade year. Specifically, the hearing officer stated the district illegally changed Bryson's programming between fifth and sixth grade, moving him from 120 minutes of service per day to 48 minutes of service per day. It is clear the district made this change without an evaluation, and the change was solely based on administrative convenience, not on the individual needs of Bryson.

The hearing officer ruled that the district is to provide Bryson services commensurate with the determinations made by a recent evaluation.

Second, the hearing officer ruled that Bryson was due compensatory education due to the lack of provision of appropriate services for his sixth-grade year. The determination of compensatory education was made by calculating two hours per day for a year, subtracted by what he was already provided, which totaled 225 hours due to Bryson.

BRYSON: SPECIAL EDUCATION
ADMINISTRATOR RESPONSE

Change of placement is a term that we hear often in the world of special education. Many people believe this means a location. This may or may not be the case. Placement is the group of services a student receives that makes up his or her special education program. A "change of placement" is a change in the educational program. Therefore, anytime the IEP is changed the "placement" has been changed. This is the case whether or not the student goes to the same location as before to receive those services. We hear change of placement discussed the most when discussing disciplinary removals. In this case, Bryson did not have disciplinary removals that brought a change of placement to the forefront; it is the parents concern that the decrease in services changed his placement in such a way that it was no longer appropriate. The school is also proposing a change in placement, with Bryson attending a classroom that is specific to students with emotional disturbance.

The district proposing to change Bryson's placement by decreasing his services, which is usually done at a time when the student has developed the skills needed to be placed in the least restrictive environment to be successful, was incongruent with this idea. Based on the information provided from the independent educational evaluation, the district may have needed to take into consideration the completion of a functional behavior assessment in conjunction with the psychological and academic assessments. Keep in mind that the purpose of a functional behavior assessment is to determine the function of the behavior. With a completed FBA, the team would have had more information to base a decision on when considering if Bryson's behavior was due to frustration (because he didn't have the skills needed to perform in the current setting), or if it was due to other emotional needs that were not being met. Based on the facts provided, there was no data to support the decision to decrease his services and to then suggest he be moved to an alternate setting. There appears to be a need for more interventions and data to determine the function of Bryson's behaviors.

The district's argument regarding the parent's agreeing to the IEP is interesting. Keep in mind that districts have the responsibility to provide free appropriate public education in the least restrictive environment, and when a student with a disability is not being successful in the current placement there then needs to be further assessment, intervention, and data to determine what the additional need is and what services need to be put in place. A district is not meeting its obligation for a least restrictive environment if the student is not being successful in the current placement, even though the student may be with their general education peers. The LRE requirement is met when the student is in a setting allowing them to be successful *and* participate with their peers to the greatest extent possible. When a student with a disability is not being successful in his or her current placement, that should then trigger the IEP team to look into changing that placement, basing the decision on data and not only information that is currently available. IDEA clearly states in §300.115 that each district must ensure "a continuum of alternative placements is available to meet the needs of children with disabilities for special education and related services." Therefore, the district needs to explore all placement options within their buildings and in other physical settings to meet the student's needs. In the case of Bryson, there appears to be a lack of evidence that this was done.

BRYSON: DISTRICT ATTORNEY RESPONSE

One of the first things that jumps out about Bryson's case is that, despite demonstrating problems with coping, social skills, and anger management, the district's identification of issues is limited to a learning disability warranting the receipt of speech and language services. The other problem for the district is the fact that Bryson's special education services were significantly reduced between fifth and sixth grade. The district's rationalization for the reduction in services does not seem logical given the additional challenges that usually come from the transition to the next academic grade. Additionally, there is nothing in the district's description of this case to suggest that it changed Bryson's IEP in an appropriate manner.

From a school district perspective, a case like Bryson's is especially difficult for a teacher and building principal to deal with, due to the disruption and fear some of the student's behaviors are likely to create. When a student throws a desk at teacher, this poses a legitimate physical threat to other students and teachers. The reservoir of empathy that teachers and even other parents might have for a child such as Bryson tends to evaporate as individuals become anxious and fearful about what might happen next. Districts can also become frustrated with their legal counsel when there is a perception that the district is powerless to deal with a disruptive or potentially violent student, while a student without an IEP would be subject to swift and decisive discipline for such behavior.

There are a couple of key things missing from the fact pattern underlying Bryson's case. The first issue is whether there were any efforts to identify and address the root cause of Bryson's behaviors or make any effort to de-escalate those behaviors before he threw the desk. The second issue is whether there was any effort on the part of the IEP team to determine whether the behaviors were a manifestation of his disability or whether there was something new that needed to be addressed. The district seemed to jump to the conclusion that Bryson needed to attend a different school.

School districts are not without options in attempting to deal with a disruptive student. If the district in this case had made an effort to determine the cause of the behavior by conducting a behavioral assessment and following up with a behavioral intervention plan, the district would be in a better position to make the call regarding whether Bryson needed to attend a different school. Placement in a different school might have been warranted, but it is hard to know prior to other steps being taken.

Because Bryson seems to do well in math but struggles with reading, this should alert the district that something may have been missed in a prior evaluation. There is further support for this premise based on teacher comments that make it sound like Bryson has struggled with reading for some time and has been promoted to the next grade without serious issues being addressed. Because he has advanced to the sixth grade, those difficulties are probably more apparent on the surface. This could also be a reason for the outbursts and would explain why Bryson had such an outburst in front of a substitute who would have been unfamiliar with those issues. Finally, the award of compensatory education is baffling to me, because it still seems unclear what Bryson should have been provided in the way of services. The number of hours resulting from a compensatory education award is supposed to have some correlation to the denial of FAPE. This correlation is not evident in the facts presented.

BRYSON: PARENT ATTORNEY RESPONSE

A twelve-year-old throwing a desk at a teacher usually garners a strong response. Unfortunately, it is not always the correct response. The initial reaction is to suggest that the student needs to be educated somewhere else. Instead, the reaction should be a strong curiosity by the adults in the child's life to understand why the child is throwing desks. Only after understanding why can those same adults play a meaningful role in helping the child manage his own behavior.

Throwing desks does not appear to be an uncommon behavior of concern. Parents often share fears of their child being labeled a monster who needs to be removed from school. As stakeholders in children's education, the IEP team needs to avoid the instinct to run from the "destructive monster" and make an effort to understand why the behavior is occurring.

Here, the district had all the information necessary to start understanding Bryson. The teacher's own comments indicate that Bryson's academic and behavior needs were not being addressed. If these concerns were expressed outside of the IEP, they did not have the desired effect. Instead, Bryson's special education time was cut in half. While we may not throw a desk, I imagine we would all be frustrated spending time in a classroom where we did not understand what was being discussed and lacked the ability to more appropriately express that frustration.

Finally, changes to IEPs should be supported by data and educational best practices. Statements like "now that he is in middle school, the specific requirements of the curriculum prevent his being educated at the same level" show the district was attempting to fit Bryson into a prepackaged program. As a result, the hearing officer viewed the change in services as a convenience for the district.

Case Eight: Conner

Communication with School

BACKGROUND

Conner, a five-year-old student who currently attends his local primary school, is in a full-time classroom for students with autism. The class is using the Applied Behavior Analysis curriculum to guide his schooling. His current services include special classroom instruction for students with autism, speech therapy, and occupational therapy. Conner has a history of significant developmental delays in the cognitive, communication, socialization, self-help, and fine motor areas. He has been diagnosed with pica. Consequently, he demonstrates adaptive behavior needs across all domains. Most notably, Conner has very limited verbal communication skills and severe limitations in his social functioning; however, since the start of kindergarten, Conner's communication has greatly increased, as has his tolerance of peers and adults throughout the school day.

Conner responds to adult-initiated interactions more and more each day, with some prompting. He is more frequently telling adults and peers, "hello" and "bye" in the hallway and during class. He is making more consistent eye contact with adults or peers speaking to him and is more consistently following requests from adults. Currently he has thirty-five motor imitations. Recently, Conner seemed to gain more of an awareness of others in his surroundings, as he now imitates the sounds and words of others with no prompting. He is also very aware of his schedule and has limited behavioral issues when transitioning from one activity to the next.

He needs light-touch hand assistance for cutting and pasting activities. Conner completes these activities while sitting in a height-appropriate seat with a back. He averages fifteen minutes before needing a one-minute sensory break.

Throughout the fifteen minutes, he is reinforced with tangible sensory items that he prefers, such as twirlers.

Conner has been working on material sorts in the classroom as he builds his vocabulary. He has also been working on identifying numbers and letters. He can spell his first and last name on most days with no prompts. He does have a terrific memory and sometimes will spell "Conner" when it is on the Wheeler match. With the partial verbal prompt "w" he spells Wheeler correctly. He can, on most days, say the letters of his name when teacher hands them to him out of order. He matches his letters in his name very well! He can also count from one to ten, with partial verbal prompts at times. He has daily practice with colors and shapes as well, and in identifying these he also needs the use of a partial verbal prompt.

During all instruction, Conner takes sensory breaks when needed. His tolerance to remain at his table during instruction has greatly increased and averages fifteen minutes. Currently a beeper is used to signal Conner when his one-minute break is over and it is time to get back to work. Conner has limited behavioral issues when keeping the consistency of the beeper and picture cards/schedule. Sensory breaks include but are not limited to: swinging, laying in the beanbag chair, playing with a peanut bounce ball, and using twirlers. To express his feelings when upset, Conner has grabbed at and bitten others.

To work on Conner's proper expressive communication, the IEP team discussed having multiple modes of communication with the parents. The parents said if there was no progress in three to four months, they should be notified and, as a team, the parents and school would explore using technology to help Conner.

Specifically, the parents stated that since Conner is nonverbal, in order for them to assist with his programming, they need updates from the school so they can help with work at home. Before Conner started kindergarten, the parents and the teachers (along with the director of special education) agreed to the following:

1. Summary of the day's activities and Conner's behavior
2. Prompt response by the district employees to emails and phone calls
3. Opportunities for the parents to come and observe activities in the classroom

About two weeks into the school year, the parents called the president of the school board, complaining that they were not being included in the activities of their son, and therefore they were unable to support him during his transition to kindergarten. They requested an immediate meeting to address their complaints.

The meeting was scheduled for the next day. The director of special education stated that everything agreed to prior to kindergarten was being implemented. The parents stated they were not receiving enough information, and that responses to emails were sometimes taking up to a day. Specifically, the daily response sheet provided to the parents (and all the other parents of students in the program) only had a few sentences and did not describe or list the activities Conner engaged in during the course of the day.

The team agreed to expand upon the sheet by listing the activities. The team also agreed to respond to all emails from the parents before they went home at the end of the day so that there were no lingering questions.

Two weeks later, the parents called the director of special education stating that they were still not receiving enough information about what was going on in school with their son, and again asked for an immediate meeting.

A meeting was scheduled for two days later. At the meeting, the parents said they liked the list, but they had no idea of Conner's progress or whether he was doing well during the activities. They asked if a checkmark or indicator could be added beside each activity to help determine if he did well or had problems during specific activities. The district agreed and said that it would be implemented in two days (the teacher was out the next day at a training). The parents asked if there was any way that emails sent in the morning could be replied to by lunchtime, and emails in the afternoon could be replied to at the end of the day. The district agreed.

About two weeks later, the parents again contacted the director of special education, stating they were still not aware of what was going on in school with their son and would like to have an immediate meeting. The district arranged to have a meeting two days later with the parents, the teacher, the principal, and the director of special education. The parents sought to have narrative descriptions of Conner's behavior during each activity, because the checkmarks and teacher-added smiley faces did little to help them understand what was going on in the classroom. The parents also asked that if they were to call the school they would get a call back from a teacher. Similar to the arrangement on emails, they requested that calls in the morning be returned by lunch, and calls in the afternoon be returned by the end of the day. The team agreed to this level of communication.

About three weeks later, the parents again contacted the director of special education, stating they did not feel they were receiving enough information about Conner's education to help them be informed and participatory parents. A meeting was scheduled for three days later. The parents stated they liked the new narratives, but they needed more information. Specifically, for activities that lasted an hour, they requested a narrative summary of every twenty minutes of Conner's activities, as well as his behaviors during those activities. The parents also requested the direct phone number for the classroom. The district agreed to implement these requests.

About three weeks later the parents contacted the director of special education requesting an immediate meeting to discuss ways of being in more contact with Conner's teachers and school staff. A meeting was scheduled for two days later. Specifically, the parents sought the cellphone number of Conner's teacher so that they could text with her during the course of the day. The teacher said she had no problems giving out her cellphone number, and the district agreed to this as well.

About a month later, the parents contacted the president of the school board, complaining about the teacher's lack of response to their texts. The parents had texted the teacher and she did not respond until two days later, and they viewed this as unacceptable. The teacher reported that she went away for the weekend without taking her cellphone, the texts the parents were referencing (there were thirty of them) were sent on Saturday morning, and there was no emergency at the time.

The director of special education and the parents held a meeting shortly after that, and discussed the following items:

1. The teacher (and staff) were very overwhelmed by having to write a paragraph on Conner's behavior and activities every twenty minutes.
2. The amount of texts sent to the teacher was overwhelming.
3. The calls to the classroom during the day were preventing instruction from occurring.

The district asked to have the amount of written information provided to the parents during the course of the day reduced to a morning summary and an afternoon summary, along with any special notices. They also asked that the parents to only call the school's central office and leave messages, and to stop texting with the teacher.

The parents did not agree to the demands and said they expected the last agreed upon behavior to continue.

DISTRICT POSITION

The district filed a due process hearing request seeking to clarify what their obligations were in keeping the parents informed about their child's progress during the day, and the level and types of acceptable communication made between the parents and the teacher. They said they were more than willing to provide a morning summary, an afternoon summary, and notices of special events. They also said that all emails and phone messages would be responded to in a timely fashion, except if there were an emergency, in which case they would respond as soon as possible.

PARENTS' POSITION

The parents argued that this level of communication is necessary. Their son is basically nonverbal, has severe autism, is five-years-old, and is transitioning to kindergarten at a new school. They feel that the only way this transition can be effective is if they understand what is going on in school and they have regular and frequent opportunities to talk with the teacher to clarify the handwritten notes.

DECISION

The hearing officer ruled that the level of communication expected by the parents was excessive. Yes, Connor has issues with pica, but that does not require notes every twenty minutes, nor does it require the ability or need to talk with the teacher as frequently as requested by the parents. The hearing officer sought to help clarify what was meant by a timely response, stating that within a working day is timely, unless there are specific issues that are time sensitive (medication changes, missed lunches, or missed permissions for field trips).

CONNER: SPECIAL EDUCATION
ADMINISTRATOR RESPONSE

The issue of communication between school and families is one that comes up often. Parents have the right to be updated on what is happening at school; however, finding a balance between what the school is able to do and what families want, without adversely affecting students' education, can be a tricky problem.

In this case it is obvious the school made a good-faith effort to provide the family with the level of communication that they were requesting. However, it increased to a level that was beyond professionally appropriate.

IDEA provides very specific guidelines, but they are also very "grey." What is meant by this is the law has specific components, but it needs to be interpreted based on the specific student situation. Therefore, timely may mean different things for different students. The same can be said about the concepts of least restrictive environment and, of course, FAPE. LRE is easier for us to understand because it is the nature of the terms that they are defined based on the individual needs of the student. However, timely can be thought of in the same way as well. As the hearing officer discussed, timely for a student who has a significant health issue, for example a student having a seizure, will look different than timely for a student whose immediate safety is not a concern.

Another thing for districts to keep in mind is the emotional state of the family. In the case described here, we have a family who is caring for and has been managing programs for a child with significant needs. Up until now, this student has most likely not been out of the parents' care for more than small amounts of time. While children are still preschool aged, most of the services in which they partake include the family. For example, when a very young child receives medical therapy, her parents will be in the therapy session with her and the service provider.

This level of day-to-day, hands-on involvement will typically change dramatically if the child attends a public school. The typical school day is significantly longer than other times when the child would have previously been out of the families' direct care. This is a frightening transition for many families. The activities that a school can engage in to build relationships and keep the parents involved are endless; however, it may take some "thinking outside of the box." The district in this case appeared to be very responsive to the families' requests. However, because the requests continued to come and the family was not satisfied, it leads me to believe that it was not clearly communicated what the family truly wanted. Sometimes this happens because the family is not sure what they want until what they get "isn't right" or "isn't enough."

When this pattern emerges, one strategy that might be used is to ask the parents, "What would that look like?" In this case the administration may have asked the parents, "If you had all of the information you needed, what would that look like on a daily basis?" The family could then describe what it would look like at home and how they envisioned it being done on the schools' end. They would also need to know what it "looks like" when the student gets home and when the student is getting ready for school. This way the team could really get down to the level of detail necessary. The team may think about having the parent come in and observe at certain times on a regular basis (e.g., anytime there is a new concept introduced).

The issue presented here is a tough one to navigate. Districts often forget that they have the right to file due process as well. Most districts will not make this move due to the risk of ruining or damaging a relationship with a family. However, it is a path that can be taken.

CONNER: DISTRICT ATTORNEY RESPONSE

In this case study, the demands of Conner's parents are understandable on a human level. Many parents worry about their child's transition to kindergarten. In all likelihood, the demands of Conner's parents are driven by parental anxiety about the well-being of their child rather than the legal responsibilities of the district. In such circumstances, it is important for districts to be careful about fostering unrealistic expectations regarding what the district is obligated to do versus what the district is willing to try to help the parents make the transition.

A reading of this fact pattern shows a district that is trying to help the parents feel more comfortable with Conner being in kindergarten. Interestingly, many of the requests have more to do with providing updates to the parents on what Conner is doing in class, rather than providing FAPE. In other words, the demands are really more parent-centered rather than student-centered, which is the focus of providing FAPE. The requests for the constant updates and immediate return of phone calls are not normally required under IDEA. Additionally, it is unsustainable given the level of legal responsibility the district has for other students. However, it is understandable why the district would go so far in acquiescing to the demands of the parents. Especially at the kindergarten level, a district wants to try to establish a good relationship with parents to build trust and avoid protracted special education litigation in the future. While there is nothing wrong with that philosophical approach, districts must be careful about staying focused on their legal obligations and sound educational practice versus placating parents early on.

Another significant issue in this case study is the impact that the contact the parents had with the president of the school board seemed to have. Many parents may know that a school board has some legal authority. Therefore, school board members are frequently approached with the expectation that they will solve the problem in the way a manager would direct employees. That expectation is often misplaced and exacerbated by the way a school board member might handle such requests. After the president of the school board was approached by the parents with a complaint the first time, the president of the school board should have politely directed the parents to speak with the superintendent or the director of special education. Intervention by a school board member is misplaced in such a situation and can cause problems for a district down the road.

The district's approach of filing for a due process hearing request is an interesting preemptory measure. Presumably, educators in the district probably thought the demands of the parents would continue to escalate. The hearing officer's decision has a sound basis in the law and seems reasonable under the circumstances.

CONNER: PARENT ATTORNEY RESPONSE

Clearly, the hearing officer was correct in ruling that a teacher didn't need to instantly respond to text messages from parents. Such a standard would guarantee the elimination of any teaching actually occurring during the day. However, the facts also show a dysfunctional IEP team that failed to collaborate on this issue.

This case would have benefited from a stronger LEA voice in the IEP team meetings. Each time the communication plan was altered it was to meet the demands of the parents. There was no discussion about how to make a communication plan that worked for everyone involved. Instead of collaborating on a solution, the LEA became a yes-man to the parent's ever-increasing demands. Despite continually increasing levels of communication, the team and the parents never had an opportunity to understand one another.

Despite numerous references to emails and text messages, there is only one reference to the parents observing activities in the classroom. This single reference was in the plan agreed to before the school year started. This was a missed opportunity. Before giving out a teacher's cell phone number, the team should have scheduled an observation for the parents. Had they seen the teacher in action, the parents may have independently concluded the expected level of communication was unworkable and unnecessary.

It should not take five levels of escalation in the communication plan to know that it is not working for both parties. No matter how much the teacher communicated with the parents, they would have always demanded more. The parents needed to see how their requested communication was interfering with their son's ability to receive an education. The teacher's belated protests were unlikely to quiet the parents' concerns. The district's acquiescence to the parents increasing demands had likely emboldened the parents' behavior. Only seeing the interference with their son's education was likely to change their minds.

Case Nine: Layla

Behavioral Issues

BACKGROUND

Layla is a kindergarten student eligible for special education and related services as a student with speech and language impairment. Layla also has some behavior problems. About halfway through the course of her kindergarten year, the district commenced additional testing and determined that she continued to be eligible for speech, but had a secondary disability of an emotional and behavioral disorder. Her special education programming during the year consisted of speech and language services twice a week for twenty minutes each time, and services for her issues related to her behavior occurred once a week for thirty minutes each time. Despite having significant behavioral issues and clear documentation of problems, the district did not want to identify her primary disability as an emotional or behavioral disorder, as she was young for kindergarten and had not attended a preschool, so her interactions in a structured setting had been limited. The parents liked this because they wanted Layla included full time in the regular kindergarten program, and agreed to limited pull out for the speech services and a once a week meeting with the emotional and behavioral disorders teacher.

Here are a few comments from the teacher's evaluation:

Layla's teacher reported she is a strong student. However, Layla seeks individualized attention from adults in the classroom, and she often calls out loudly and inappropriately during lessons. She has difficulty making close friendships with peers and abiding by personal boundary rules, often invading the personal space of peers and adults, particularly females. Layla has difficulty following directives given by adults and will often ignore or do the opposite of what she has been told. At times Layla's body language suggests that she is not paying attention to the teacher; however, she is able to answer questions about the lesson despite her perceived lack of attention.

A district social worker completed a social work evaluation on Layla. The team that completed the questionnaires identified some areas of emotion as strengths for Layla. She does not struggle with sadness, unhappiness, or worry/fears while at school. Layla struggles with conduct, hyperactivity, peers, and prosocial skills. Layla struggles with what to do when she becomes frustrated or angry. She also has difficulty with peer interactions. She seeks attention from others, but not always with positive behaviors. She struggles with keeping her body calm and is oftentimes observed as restless. At this time, the IEP team may wish to consider additional supports for Layla for direct instruction in social skills.

An FBA was completed. Areas of concern include Layla becoming physically aggressive, verbally aggressive, and noncompliant with directives. Her physical aggression can look like hitting, kicking, pushing others, and throwing items. Layla's verbal aggression can involve yelling or screaming and can be directed toward another person. She has also been observed as noncompliant to directives by refusing to complete a task, refusing to follow a direction given by a teacher or another adult, and refusing to stop an action after being directed to do so. The summary hypothesis is that when presented with a redirection to task, Layla will become noncompliant to directives in order to attempt to avoid the task demand.

Her teacher completed the Behavior Assessment System for Children, Third Edition (BASC-3). The following concerns fell within the clinically significant range on the Clinical Scale: hyperactivity, aggression, externalizing problems, depression, and behavioral symptoms index. The parents did not complete the form.

PARENTS' POSITION

The parents expressed that Layla does not demonstrate these behaviors at home. While she does play rough with her older siblings and seeks attention from her parents, it does not cause problems at home. The parents agreed that additional supports could be put into place in school; however, they expressed concern regarding pulling her out of her regular education classroom more than absolutely necessary.

Starting in March of that year, Layla's behaviors started to deteriorate. This is a summary of the behaviors Layla demonstrated during one two-hour observation:

During the time I observed Layla, there was a crisis that involved other teachers, with Layla having to be removed to a different classroom. They indicated to me that this happens three or more times a week. I also observed an aide and a special education teacher work to help her remain on task in class, with limited success.

Layla is a very impulsive and inattentive student who likes to negotiate. However, it is the impulsivity that seems to cause the most problems in her participation in the classroom. She grabs whatever is near, she darts around the classroom, she throws whatever she can get her hands on, she climbs on the desks and on tables. This is just in the kindergarten classroom. She does not like to be told no. She loves attention, seeming to be reinforced equally from positive as well as negative attention.

In talking with the teacher, it was indicated to me that she has problems with transitions. That may be the case. It looks like Layla has problems just doing what is asked of her when it does not involve what she wants to do at that moment.

The other students in her class seem mildly oblivious to her behavior, but I would be very concerned about her impulsivity, as I saw her hit two different teachers, pull one teacher's ponytail, and pull another teacher's tie. She also threw a chair, and was grabbing for others' things to throw before they were taken from her. She tried to pull the special education teacher's sweater and the lanyard of another teacher, and tried to kick several teachers.

You have a child who when upset engages in impulsive acts that very well may cause harm to other students in her classroom.

Behaviors I saw include running, hitting teachers, hitting walls, throwing items, noncompliance, and trying to argue with the teachers.

After a week of incidents where Layla pushed the bus driver (while the bus was in motion), punched a teacher, kicked the aide, and punched two different students in the stomach, the district sought to have her moved to a more restrictive placement. The more restrictive placement was at a different school in the district, and the parents wanted her educated in the same building as her brother, who is nondisabled and is in first grade.

DISTRICT POSITION

At the due process hearing, the district presented evidence of the issues Layla has in class. Layla needed to be removed from her kindergarten class every single day for a two-month period; this was despite the additional supports that were provided to her. These additional supports included modifying the positive behavior support plan to include the following steps:

1. Adding tiered positive reinforcement, tangible reinforcers, and an updated reinforcement survey
2. Creating a personal schedule, binder, social stories (scripts), and checklists
3. Adding mandatory breaks to Layla's schedule (Where? How often? What is appropriate for during breaks?)
4. Group guidance
5. Pre-teaching and priming for transitions/decision-making
6. Linking choices to positive reinforcement
7. Avoiding power struggles
8. Clearly defining a safety plan
9. Providing paraprofessional support in the afternoon and at all recesses
10. Providing support to facilitate social skills
11. Providing support for Layla's teacher

The district stated that even with these steps, Layla was still having severe problems, many of which involved aggression toward teachers and support staff.

The parents argued that she was not identified as a student needing services for emotional and behavioral disorders, only identified as eligible for speech and language services. Yes, she does have some behavioral problems; however, the district had not sought to identify her as a student with a disability other than speech language needs. Additionally, since the district was proposing to place in her in different school, away from her friends and her brother, and involving a longer drive to and from school, this was not the least restrictive environment for her, and enough supports and training had not been provided to allow her to function in her current kindergarten classroom.

The district responded that when they evaluated Layla, the parents did not want her labeled as emotionally disturbed, and that she had not participated in a preschool program, was young for her class, and they were hesitant to label her as emotionally disturbed at such a young age, despite the overwhelming evidence. Additionally, though she was only labeled as eligible for speech and language services, she was found eligible for special education, and the label does not dictate level or placement; that is a decision of the IEP team.

DECISION

The hearing officer admonished the district for acquiescing to the parent's demands for the label of the disability. The hearing officer did acknowledge that Layla was eligible for special education and related services as a student with a speech language impairment; however, the behaviors that she manifested indicated that she required additional support. The district did not make the case as to why she needed to be moved to a different school, other than for administrative convenience. The district did not try to increase the services for Layla at her current school, other than the positive behavior support plan and the addition of a paraprofessional in the afternoon and at recess. There are many other behavioral supports that should be tried before sending Layla to a different school. The hearing officer also questioned the training of the paraprofessional. Did the paraprofessional have training in dealing with a crisis? Reducing behaviors? Not escalating behaviors? Did the paraprofessional have hands-on training? This was not indicated as a part of the hearing.

Finally, the hearing officer stated that there needs to be data on the amount of Layla's behaviors, including frequency and duration, and data on the implementation of the positive behavior support plan.

LAYLA: SPECIAL EDUCATION ADMINISTRATOR RESPONSE

The continuum of placements and least restrictive environment placement is the topic this school team needs to discuss. IDEA requires each district to offer a continuum of placements. What this means in practical terms is that there needs to be a wide range of services available and therefore attempted or at least considered in order to provide students free appropriate public education in their least restrictive environment. As discussed in earlier cases, a "placement" refers to the services provided and not necessarily the location of the services. In the case of Layla, as the facts are presented, it does not appear that the district has considered a full continuum of placements. In this case it appears this team did not attempt much in terms of other placement options (for example, different services or instruction) during Layla's kindergarten year. If there were behavioral concerns, interventions needed to be attempted and a full continuum of placement options needed to be discussed. It appears this team only discussed two options: full-time placement in the general education classroom, or a completely different school and special education classroom full time. There is a whole continuum between these two options for consideration.

The district had made some steps in the right direction to prepare to consider other placement options; however, it appears they did not follow through with those and jumped to an alternate location. Though an alternate location might be the proper setting, documentation to provide support for the district's decision is needed. A lot of good baseline information was gathered by the social worker as well as in the FBA; however, the mere conducting of assessments is not adequate to justify moving from the least restrictive environment for education (the general education setting 100 percent of the time) to one of the most restrictive (setting in an alternate school with only students with emotional disturbance). IEP teams have it within their ability to make these decisions. However, when there is such significant disagreement between parties (the family and the school in this case), a series of placements need to be attempted, data collected, and changes made based on that data.

Another step that could have happened early on revolves around the idea of early intervention. The facts describe the team recognizing early on that Layla had some behavioral issue of which they were not sure of the source. Her history is that she had no preschool experiences and is also young for kindergarten. The team recognized that she was missing some behavioral components that would allow her to be successful in kindergarten. At that point the general education intervention process should have begun. In this process the team could have made initial steps to teach her the skills needed and/or provide some accommodations or modifications that would improve her success rate. The facts in this case do not reveal if any of these steps had been taken. IDEA requires that "(1) . . . prior to, or as part of, the referral process" a student must have been "provided appropriate instruction in regular education settings, delivered by qualified personnel; and (2) Data-based documentation of repeated assessments of achievement at reasonable intervals, reflecting formal assessment of student progress during instruction [be] provided to the child's parents" [§300.309 (b)(1)(2)].

In addition, the reauthorization of IDEA in 2004 included a provision for early intervening services: §300.226. This provision allows schools the option of using a portion (up to 15 percent) of their IDEA funds to develop and implement services to children prior to their qualifying for special education services. In reviewing the facts presented in this case, it is hard to see where many, if any, early intervening services were provided. The team conducted an FBA which gave them some great information regarding strategies to try; however, those strategies were not implemented. There is also not a lot of data to show what actual interventions were attempted. Some assessments were administered, but no changes in Layla's program appear to have been made based on the results of these assessments.

LAYLA: DISTRICT ATTORNEY RESPONSE

The hearing officer's decision in this case study is confounding and frustrating from the perspective of this school district attorney. One of the more challenging problems for public schools is the balance between providing a student with required services under IDEA and the safety of that student, other students, and school staff. Educators often feel helpless and frustrated by the perception that they are restricted from dealing with these issues in a manner that places safety first. In this case study, the district went through several steps that would have been recommended by many attorneys who represent school districts.

While it is understandable that the hearing officer was critical of the district for acquiescing to parental preferences in order to avoid labeling Layla with an emotional or behavioral disorder, the decision seems to brush aside the other steps the district took regarding the matter. The aggressive and impulsive behaviors directed at other students and staff demonstrate some real safety concerns for the district. For example, pushing the bus driver while the bus was in motion had the potential to be a catastrophic event for the driver and other students on the bus. In addition to human tragedy, the incident would have created potential liability exposure for the district if an accident occurred.

The district deserves high marks for conducting the FBA and identifying several issues that required additional support through the modification of a behavioral support plan. The reinforcements and the use of the paraprofessionals are the types of measures that attorneys typically recommend before a student is placed in an alternative setting. The district's request for a due process hearing is the right move after a district has exhausted other efforts and has reached the conclusion that a change in placement is necessary. While it is not too hard to understand why the district delayed the identification of the emotional and behavioral disorders, that decision did little to address real needs early on.

The response of the parents in this case study is not uncommon. It is frequently difficult for parents to come to grips with issues identified by educators. However, the evaluation information and repetitive number of classroom incidents seem to support the district's position that there is overwhelming evidence of emotional and behavioral issues that need to be addressed.

Another aspect of the hearing officer's decision that is hard to understand is the failure to recognize the amount of class time Layla is missing because of the constant need to remove her from class. The obligation to place a student in the least restrictive environment should be based on the appropriate placement for the student. Finally, while the training of a paraprofessional might have some relevance, the issue that should have been the focus of the decision is whether the positive behavior support plan was carried out properly by all staff involved in the plan.

LAYLA: PARENT ATTORNEY RESPONSE

Philosophers have argued for different characterizations of the value of emotions and reason in decision-making for centuries. Plato viewed reason and emotion as two horses pulling a chariot in different directions while the charioteer struggles to get them to work as a team. David Hume, however, argued that "reason is a slave to the passions." Hume argued that we project subjective feelings onto an act and call it bad if it makes us feel bad and good if it makes us feel good. The conflict between letting emotion or reason guide decision-making is confronted by educators every day.

Conclusions in evaluation reports should be dictated by reason. Here, Layla's IEP team let emotions override the reasoned conclusion of the evaluation report to the detriment of Layla and the district. Both the district and parents expressed resistance to labeling Layla as emotionally disturbed, despite overwhelming evidence. The team likely harbored negative feelings about the label and felt some sense of comfort in sparing Layla from the term. By refusing to confront the evidence, the team continued to minimize the level of support required.

The hearing officer's decision requires the team to return to data and reason to make educational decisions for Layla. The hearing officer recognized the team did not fully understand Layla's behaviors. The decision recognized a need for data on Layla's behavior and the school's intervention. It questioned the training provided to the support staff. All of these tools should help the team take a step back and develop a reason-based approach to intervening for Layla. This approach will undoubtedly incorporate the emotional engagement of the staff and student but will be done to allow the team to calibrate the response to monitoring Layla's growth.

Hopefully, the use of additional training and data will also result in an improved positive behavior support plan. Presented out of context, one wonders how anyone who participated in the eleven-step plan felt it was appropriate. The steps consist of nothing more than buzzwords, aspirational statements, and unanswered questions. Plans are usually meant to be carried out. The more people involved in a plan, the more specifics need to be included. Generalized statements leave much room for interpretation in a field that requires consistency.

The IDEA expects IEPs to be transferable. The law recognizes that families often move in the middle of a school year. The new LEA is expected to carry out the previous LEA's plan for at least a short time. Our office often poses this hypothetical at IEP meetings: How would a new school district know what to do when they receive Layla? Here the question would be unanswerable.

Case Ten: Nolan

Compensatory Education

BACKGROUND

As a part of this due process hearing, the parents are asking that the district fund an out-of-district placement. The parents argue that Nolan is entitled to tuition for out-of-district educational programming, ESY, related services, and transportation because (1) the district's proposed educational placement is not appropriate; (2) the parents' unilaterally selected placement is appropriate; and (3) there is no equitable reason not to award tuition. Nolan and his parents are further entitled to compensatory education to the fullest extent of the law because the district has failed to provide FAPE for Nolan for the entire time he has been a student in the district.

The parents allege that the district has failed to provide FAPE for Nolan since he was identified as a student in need of special education services in kindergarten.

The parents requested an IEE after the district issued its latest reevaluation. The latest evaluation reported Nolan's Full Scale Intelligence Quotient (FSIQ) score as 65–24 points below the 89 he achieved when the district last evaluated him three years ago. The district maintains that the discrepancy between Nolan's FSIQ scores could be explained by the fact that the previous evaluator had some personal issues that interfered with her ability to perform professionally. The district's reevaluation also concluded that Nolan did not have a speech/language impairment.

The parents requested the IEE because of the precipitous drop in Nolan's FSIQ score and because on recent outside testing Nolan achieved at the second-grade level in math and at the third-grade level in reading.

The independent evaluator stated that Nolan "has significant language and learning disabilities," and concluded that

Nolan is in need of language services to improve word retrieval, vocabulary, knowledge formation, grammatical usage, organization of his narrative, and listening comprehension skills. Nolan requires an academic environment where he is instructed in a small group, grouped with similarly performing peers, and taught by a special education teacher for the next year.

The parents point out the district exited Nolan from speech language services when he was in third grade without any evaluation data.

The most recent proposed IEP was provided by the district for fourth grade. It states that "Nolan will receive ninety minutes of mathematics instruction and forty-three minutes every other day of learning support study hall for reteaching and organizational skills. Three times a week Nolan will meet with a reading specialist for thirty minutes. All other times Nolan will be with regular education peers." The district went on to state that "Nolan has participation in the general education curriculum in the areas of science, social studies, and specials." The parents allege that this is not FAPE, pointing out that this is less support than he received in previous years.

The parents also have a note from a teacher stating in part:

I wanted to send you a brief note regarding a noticeable change in Nolan. Since coming back to school after the holiday break, he has shown regression in his math skills. Concepts that he knew well or questions he could easily answer prior to the break are now a struggle for him. At first, it seemed like "typical" regression that might be evident after a break from school, but he doesn't seem to be recouping those skills. There has also been a gradual decrease in attentiveness and focus in his classes. There have not been any disruptive behavior concerns at this point, though.

PARENTS' POSITION

The parents are alleging that the district cannot meet Nolan's needs and that the private school is appropriate, and argue that taking all of his subjects in a small group, with similarly performing peers taught by a special education teacher, will benefit Nolan. The district's offered programming is not FAPE.

The parents continue their argument, stating that it is equitable for the district to fund tuition at the private school. The district has failed to provide FAPE for Nolan for years. The parents have heard and carefully considered the district's offers of FAPE. The parents have actively participated in discussions with the district concerning the provision of FAPE. The IEE funded by the district concludes that Nolan needs to be in small classes with similarly developing peers, taught by a special education teacher for all subjects. The district has confirmed that it cannot provide this programming. The district is proposing that it continue to program in a manner that has not yielded meaningful progress for Nolan for years. There is no equitable reason not to award an out-of-district placement.

Additionally, the parents are seeking compensatory education. They stated a review of Nolan's educational records shows the district did not provide FAPE to Nolan. Instead, year after year, the district failed to meet Nolan's needs with IEPs that did not have baselines and measureable goals against which Nolan's progress could be monitored and properly addressed. The recent IEE shows that Nolan has not made meaningful progress.

Additionally, the district exited Nolan from speech/language services in third grade without proper evaluation. In this case, this violation is particularly egregious and detrimental, as the IEE concluded

> There is a preponderance of evidence to suggest that Nolan continues to have significant issues in the areas of language expression and comprehension. . . . Nolan is in need of language services to improve word retrieval, vocabulary knowledge, sentence formulation, grammatical usage, organization of his narrative, and listening comprehension skills.

Comments from Nolan's kindergarten teacher include the following. The kindergarten teacher reported that Nolan "does not complete class work," is "not working at grade level," and "has difficulty completing thoughts or ideas verbally." With respect to reading, she reported that Nolan had "poor comprehension skills," "difficulty with words at grade level," "difficulty reading independently," and "difficulty sequencing a story." With respect to mathematics, she reported that Nolan "has difficulty solving problems" and "fails to follow the necessary steps with equations." For writing, his kindergarten teacher reported that Nolan "fails to correctly complete sentences or thoughts in writing" and "fails to organize writing assignments."

Nolan has not made meaningful progress over the entire time he has been enrolled at the district.

First Grade

The IEP team met and set goals for reading and math. It is unclear whether or how the district determined baselines for these first-grade goals or Nolan's instructional level. It is clear that Nolan did not meet these goals. It is also clear that the district did not provide progress monitoring. In response to Nolan's failure to meet the goals in his IEP, the district did not determine Nolan's baseline or offer different programming. Instead, it included new, more advanced second-grade goals for reading and math. Additionally, after Nolan met his language goal in first grade, the district did not include a new goal for language in second grade or after. The IEP for second grade included a speech articulation goal only.

Second Grade

The pattern of no meaningful progress and no meaningful response continued in second grade. Nolan continued to fail to make progress through second grade. The district failed to make changes to Nolan's educational programming. The district did not provide quarterly progress reports. Instead, the only progress report the district has produced shows that Nolan had not met his articulation, writing, and math goals in second grade.

Third Grade

The pattern of no meaningful progress and no meaningful response continued in third grade. Nolan did not meet his goals in writing and math in third grade.

Additionally, Nolan was exited from speech and language services without a complete reevaluation report, which concluded that "Nolan has mastered the production of the (s) and (z) phonemes; he no longer has an articulation impairment and should be dismissed from speech and language." The reevaluation report did not assess Nolan's expressive and receptive language skills.

Fourth Grade

The pattern of no meaningful progress and no meaningful response continued in fourth grade. Nolan did not meet his goals in fourth grade.

Fifth Grade

The pattern of no meaningful progress and no meaningful response continued in fifth grade. In fifth grade, Nolan continued to have the same goal in math as in the three previous years. Moreover, while the goals in reading and writing were purportedly at fifth-grade level, the goals did not include baselines and cannot be squared with Nolan's level as reflected in the district's Reevaluation Report and the IEE.

Sixth Grade

The sixth-grade IEP had only one goal: "Nolan will complete the Level 4 Math Computation and Level 4 Math Concepts & Applications assessments with a minimum of 80 percent accuracy." The IEP was not FAPE.

After the IEE was submitted, the district proposed another IEP, which did not address the needs identified and was not FAPE.

Since this latest IEP, the district has begun providing speech-language services without identifying speech-language as a related service in an IEP and without issuing a plan for the services.

For the foregoing reasons, Nolan and his parents request the following relief:

1. an out-of-district placement funded by the district, including transportation and ESY;
2. compensatory education to the fullest extent permitted by law;
3. reimbursement for private tutoring expenses;
4. all other equitable remedies that are just and proper; and
5. attorneys' fees and costs.

DISTRICT RESPONSE

First Grade

Nolan did not master all of his goals, though he came extremely close. Not meeting/mastering an IEP goal does not mean that Nolan was denied FAPE. It simply means he continues to need special education and may need more supports in reading and math.

Second Grade

Nolan is very close to achieving the second-grade reading goal. The district agrees there were some issues with the math goal in second grade. Once again, not mastering the goal does not necessarily equate to a carte blanche denial of FAPE.

Third Grade

Nolan was dismissed from speech for meeting his articulation goal. He did not master his math goals, though he was close to mastering his writing goals and clearly met his reading goals. Once again, not mastering a goal does not automatically translate into a wholesale denial of FAPE.

Fourth Grade

The district once again disagreed that the pattern of no meaningful progress or no meaningful response continued in the fourth grade. While the parents indicated that Nolan did not meet his goals in fourth grade, once again, not mastering a goal does not necessarily mean that the entire year was a failure, nor was it a wholesale denial of FAPE.

Nolan met his reading goals and came close to mastering his math goals and writing goals.

Fifth Grade

The parents removed Nolan from language arts. The district stated that they could agree to disagree on the basis for this.

Nolan met his math goal for the year. The focus was getting him to Level 4 at 80 percent accuracy, which he obtained.

Sixth Grade

The district agreed that the only goal in the April IEP was that Nolan would complete the Level 4 math computation and Level 4 math concepts and applications assessment with a minimum of 80 percent accuracy.

Conclusion

The parents indicated that the district has failed to provide FAPE since the time the student started kindergarten. The district disagreed with that statement.

DECISION

The hearing officer agreed with the parents that the student was due compensatory education for two hours a day for two years, due to inappropriate services in language arts and math. The hearing officer also awarded compensatory education for speech and language services due to Nolan's inappropriate dismissal from the program, given that the district could not produce an evaluation substantiating its claim that it was completed prior to termination of services.

Finally, the hearing officer awarded tuition reimbursement for one year at the private school.

NOLAN: DISTRICT ATTORNEY RESPONSE

The summary of the hearing officer's decision in this case study seems to lack reasoning for the basis for the two years of compensatory education.

Additionally, the award of one year of private school tuition seems misplaced since it was a unilateral decision by the parents to place Nolan in a private school. Arguably, tuition should only be awarded in those cases in which the hearing officer determines that the private school is the proper placement for a student. That may very well be the case, since the district acknowledged at one point that Nolan would benefit from smaller classes and the district was unable to provide smaller classes. However, this should be based on more than speculation. If tuition reimbursement is based solely on a parental preference, this has the force and effect of operating as a *de facto* voucher to attend private school without being anchored to the requirements of IDEA.

While compensatory education is frequently thought of as an equitable remedy that is awarded based on the past transgressions of an LEA, there should be some connection between the remedy and addressing the student's needs going forward. IDEA is not a statute that specifically provides for money damages, and ordering tuition without reasoning that is relevant to addressing student needs is inconsistent with the policy objectives of IDEA. However, it seems like there are more decisions at this level that seem to apply compensatory education more broadly in cases where a district has fallen short in providing FAPE for multiple years. Unfortunately for school districts a blanket tuition reimbursement remedy seems to be all too easy for hearing officers to grant in circumstances in which parents are more satisfied with a private school setting. The missing piece of the hearing officer's analysis is whether the private school is a proper placement for the present purpose of providing FAPE.

Despite my criticism of the hearing officer's decision, from the legal perspective of a school district attorney, the district had a weaker hand to play in the hearing for a number of reasons. The anomaly with the IQ testing seems inexcusable, and one wonders why the district did not retest if there was a known personnel issue that skewed the results in the first test. Sweeping an issue under the rug seldom works very well, because it can be exposed in a due process hearing. It is also hard to defend Nolan's exit from speech-language services in the third grade without any evaluation data.

Another area of weakness in the district's position is the lack of progress in meeting goals every year. While it might be true that students will not always meet a goal that is set, the fact that Nolan consistently failed to meet goals during his entire elementary school career creates the appearance that the district exhibited a disengaged approach to the development of IEPs for several years. Nolan having the same math goal for three consecutive years reinforces that perception. Overall, the result in this case study is not well reasoned. However, this is the kind of overly broad result that can occur and that parents can use to create a narrative that a school district went on "autopilot" for several consecutive years in the development of IEPs and the delivery of FAPE.

NOLAN: PARENT ATTORNEY RESPONSE

The IEP process is ripe for complacency. Completing the document and getting parent approval masks the awareness of actual deficiencies. The likelihood of passing the deficiencies along to the next year is increased by the ease of cutting and pasting the previous year's IEP contents. The team approach causes the IEP team to lose some sense of personal ownership over the document. Many of these concerns may go undetected for years without any protest from the parents.

When I am unjustifiably accused of a wrongdoing, I see what objective evidence I have available to justify my actions. Ideally, the evidence exists in writing and was shared with my accuser before the dispute arose. There is no strong evidence to prevent or prevail in a dispute.

Recently, I received a text message from an unknown number in the middle of the night. It read "Going on 2 years. No word. If ur not gonna do anything I'd like what I gave to you back please." After asking who the message was sent from, the messenger identified himself as a potential client I had met with two years ago but hadn't spoken to since. I responded that I agreed two years was a long time and asked if he had tried to reach out during those two years. I searched my email and found a chain of emails from me, with no response from the potential client. I sent him a copy and he calmed down. If I had not had that documented communication, I would have had little to defend myself with. I did not remember the meeting or the client.

LEAs that follow the processes and procedures required in the IDEA should have no problem accessing a wealth of evidence to defend an unjustified claim. Special education is a very document-driven process. We have reports, notices, and plans to cover every aspect of a child's education. We just have to fill them out faithfully and with the correct information.

Here Nolan's LEA's well of evidence was dry. There was no evaluation to justify the removal of speech and language support. Nolan had the same goals in math for four consecutive years. The goals were not based on baseline data and were not corresponding with Nolan's evaluation report results. The district disagreed with the parents' claim of a denial of FAPE since kindergarten but had little evidence to support that position.

Case Eleven: Zander

Autism/Behavioral Issues

BACKGROUND

Zander is a fourteen-year-old eighth-grade student eligible for special education with a primary disability of autism. He currently receives full-time instruction from a special education teacher for his autism. He is supported through the use of a teacher's assistant, assistive technology (iPad), direct instruction with a classroom teacher, speech five times a week, and occupational therapy for eighteen hours per marking period.

In third grade, the nonverbal portion of the Stanford-Binet Intelligence Scales, Fifth Edition was administered to assess Zander's intellectual potential. He scored a nonverbal score of 42. It is important to note this score should be interpreted with a great deal of caution, as a variety of components such as Zander's ability to communicate, his fine motor ability, his frustration tolerance level, and a question of potential color blindness may affect the validity of the obtained score. As such, this assessment should be interpreted by examining Zander's performance on the individual tasks required of him.

In Zander's verbal behavior program, he is currently receiving intensive teaching on ten programs. The programs include manding, motor imitation, receptive identification of common objects, matching shapes, receptive number identification, receptive body part identification, receptive color identification, matching common objects to sample, receptive capital letter identification, and matching upper case/lower case letters.

There is an extensive medical history that has had a significant impact on Zander's ability to function within the educational setting. Zander was the result of a full-term pregnancy. His development followed a normal progression until he started to regress at sixteen months old. Zander was diagnosed with a pervasive developmental disorder (PDD) at twenty-three months before being diagnosed with autism at three years old. Zander suffers from significant pressure headaches and has also been diagnosed with a Chiari malformation. According to cappskids.org, Chiari malformations (CMs) are

> structural defects in the cerebellum, the part of the brain that controls balance. Normally the cerebellum and parts of the brain stem sit in an indented space at the lower rear of the skull, above the foramen magnum (a funnel-like opening to the spinal canal). When part of the cerebellum is located below the foramen magnum, it is called a Chiari malformation. CMs may develop when the bony space is smaller than normal, causing the cerebellum and brain stem to be pushed downward into the foramen magnum and into the upper spinal canal. The resulting pressure on the cerebellum and brain stem may affect functions controlled by these areas and block the flow of cerebrospinal fluid (CSF)—the clear liquid that surrounds and cushions the brain and spinal cord—to and from the brain.
>
> Individuals with CM may complain of neck pain, balance problems, muscle weakness, numbness or other abnormal feelings in the arms or legs, dizziness, vision problems, difficulty swallowing, ringing or buzzing in the ears, hearing loss, vomiting, insomnia, depression, or headache made worse by coughing or straining. Hand coordination and fine motor skills may be affected. Symptoms may change for some individuals, depending on the buildup of CSF and result-ing pressure on the tissues and nerves. . . . Infants may have symptoms from any type of CM and may have difficulty swallowing, be irritable when being fed, have excessive drooling, a weak cry, gagging or vomiting, arm weakness, a stiff neck, breathing problems, developmental delays, and an inability to gain weight.[1]

Zander has had a series of surgeries to alleviate pressure, insert shunts, and repair damage from the CM. In elementary school, he suffered from severe anxiety that prevented him from attending school. A chaining program was put into place in order to get him to attend school. Medically related difficul-ties have continued to have an impact on Zander's ability to participate in the educational setting in middle school. In terms of adaptive functioning, Zander has limited verbal communication and motor skills. He works to develop daily living skills as part of his curriculum.

DISTRICT POSITION

The reason for the due process hearing is that Zander has not been attend-ing school on a regular basis, and though the district feels they can provide

---

1. https://www.cappskids.org/chiari-malformation/

FAPE, they are not being given a chance to do so. Additionally, the parents have sent a bill to the district for private occupational therapy services that the district does not feel is either warranted or necessary.

Specifically, every Monday, Wednesday, and Friday for the past year, if Zander came to school, he did not arrive until around noon. On those mornings, the parents report they are taking him to see a private occupational therapist (OT) that works with him for three intensive hours. Additionally, when he does come to school, the only way he will get out of the car to come into school (based on his parents' report) is if they provide him with a twenty-piece Chicken McNuggets and a large soft drink.

The district stated that on the days he goes to see the private OT, he is extremely tired and not able to work the rest of the day. Additionally, given that he has ingested a large number of calories just prior to entering school, edibles are not reinforcing to Zander.

The district stated that they are seeking that the hearing officer order they are not liable for the private occupational therapy sessions, given they are willing to provide multiple OT sessions themselves. The district stated that if the parents want to continue with the private OT they are fine with it and will work closely with the provider. However, they are requesting the parents schedule the private OT so as not to interrupt school and have Zander miss as many hours in a given week as he does.

The district provided evidence that the certifications of the OT they employ were the same as the Zander's private OT, and that their training was essentially the same. They were also able to provide data on progress Zander was making on the Tuesdays and Thursdays that he was in school.

Both sides stipulated that Zander clearly has a lot of needs that should be addressed relating to his autism diagnosis and the CM.

PARENTS' POSITION

The parents responded by stating they feel the private OT is absolutely necessary for Zander to make progress. They also stated that they do not have problems with what the district is offering as a part of their program, especially the occupational therapy services. However, Zander has multiple issues that the private OT is working to address and they do not feel they can pay for the services. The private OT is only available in the mornings, as he sees other clients during the course of the day. The parents also stated that they were amenable to developing a behavior plan that would get Zander out of the car and reduce the amount of food necessary. But they were adamant that the district pay for the private occupational therapy services.

DECISION

The hearing officer, though sympathetic to the parents' plight, ruled that the district was not obligated to pay for the private occupational therapy services. The hearing officer could not order the parents to seek Medicaid reimbursement for the private occupational therapy services, but suggested that this be considered.

ZANDER: SPECIAL EDUCATION ADMINISTRATOR RESPONSE

In the case of Zander, it appears the crux of the issue is revolving around the outside occupational therapy and the parents' inability to pay for that medical service. It is important to have a discussion regarding the purpose of related services for IDEA. There are many times students require additional medical services outside of those supported in IDEA. Section §300.34 discusses related services. IDEA states that the purpose of related services is "to assist a child with a disability to benefit from special education" [§300.34(a)]. Related services include:

> transportation and such developmental, corrective, and other supportive services . . . [such as] speech-language pathology and audiology services, interpreting services, psychological services, physical and occupational therapy, recreation, including therapeutic recreation, early identification and assessment of disabilities in children, counseling services, including rehabilitation counseling, orientation and mobility services, and medical services for diagnostic or evaluation purposes. Related services also include school health services and school nurse services, social work services in schools and parent counseling and training. [§300.34(a)]

The guidance goes on to clarify that the list provided in the law "is not exhaustive and may include other developmental, corrective, or supportive services if they are required to assist a child with a disability to benefit from special education. It would be impractical to list every service that could be a related service."[2]

It is important that the purpose of related services is to allow a student to benefit from their special education program. This concept is often misunderstood by families, advocates, and general education staff. Families, advocates,

---

2. https://sites.ed.gov/idea/files/finalregulations.pdf

and general education staff often request related services extending beyond what is required for a student to benefit from their special education program and this often becomes an area of contention. One way to help others understand the purpose of related services in IDEA is to think of curb cuts. Curb cuts allow those who would not otherwise have access to the sidewalks to access them. They do not necessarily give access to all sidewalks, but to particular sidewalks. Related services that go beyond what is needed for students to benefit from their educational program are then the responsibility of the medical field and the family. IDEA is very clear in the requirement that schools are responsible only for the services required for the student to benefit from their special education program.

Based on the idea that FAPE looks very different for each student with a disability, the responsibility falls on the IEP team to determine what is interfering with the student accessing and benefiting from their special education program.

ZANDER: DISTRICT ATTORNEY RESPONSE

From the vantage point of a school district attorney, the hearing officer correctly decided that the district should not be responsible for paying for private occupational therapy services under the facts presented. However, there is a major missing legal component to both the district's position regarding private occupational therapy and the hearing officer's decision. Occupational therapy services are typically provided under Section 504 of the Rehabilitation Act rather than IDEA, and there is not a single reference to Section 504 as a consideration in the case study. The decision demonstrates the problem of focusing a great deal of attention on the services provided under IDEA while forgetting that a student may require accommodations under Section 504.

At a minimum, Zander's physical issues demonstrate the need for the district to conduct an evaluation to determine if Section 504 accommodations are warranted. The CM diagnosis should easily meet the criteria of a 504 disability. Additionally, the symptoms of the condition are so varied and serious that a Section 504 team that included a school nurse should have met to determine what kinds of accommodations Zander would require in order to attend school on a regular basis. This conclusion is supported by the fact that Zander is not attending school on a regular basis and the facts strongly suggest this is due in large measure to the medical issues related to the CM.

A Section 504 evaluation and plan should address those issues related to the disability that may be preventing Zander from benefiting from his public education. In addition to dealing with the medical issues, the agreement should also address the need and the amount of occupational therapy. Moreover, the parents and the private occupational therapist should not be making a decision that prevents Zander's attendance at school while the district takes a "hands-off" approach to the issue. Because the district will be required to provide accommodations under Section 504, the district should be taking the lead in evaluating the student and determining how to provide access to the school's programs and services.

While the parents will have an active role in the development of the 504 plan, the parents should not be making a unilateral determination that Zander cannot be at school based on the availability of a private occupational therapy instructor. The legal standard should be focused on the reasonable accommodations necessary for Zander to access district services and programs. It should not be focused on the availability of a specific private therapist. Finally, until the district conducts an evaluation to determine Zander's need for occupational therapy services, the parents and the district will remain in the dark about the extent to which those services can be provided during instructional time or provided as a wraparound service. Even though the district prevailed in this case, it would be advisable to go back to the drawing board to address potential issues under Section 504.

ZANDER: PARENT ATTORNEY RESPONSE

The hearing officer clearly reached the correct conclusion. Districts should not be subject to parents' bills for private services that the district can provide. However, I believe the district could have handled the situation in a way that may have prevented the issue from maturing into a due process hearing.

I am curious what the district was doing during the year that Zander attended school for half the day, three times a week. I suspect the attendance office was happily accepting medical excuses that unknowingly encouraged the parents to continue this pattern. It is my opinion that the district should have done more to force a discussion about the appropriateness of this practice. Had the district approached the parents a month into the Monday/Wednesday/ Friday schedule the parents may have been more willing to abandon it and listen to alternatives.

At age fourteen, Zander is also approaching the IDEA's mandatory transition planning age and has already met the lower age requirement enacted by many states. This is a prime opportunity for the district to be teaching the family about the use of outside agencies and how they can scaffold supports to work with the IEP team to meet Zander's needs. If the district was able to sell themselves as the appropriate quarterback to coordinate Zander's services, the parents wouldn't be worried about paying an outside OT to provide those same services.

While the conclusion is correct, the process the parties went through to get to it is disappointing. The IDEA and its regulations provide ample procedures and processes to allow teams to get ahead of potential concerns like these. A proactive IEP team may have prevented this dispute and almost certainly would have shortened it.

Case Twelve: Mason

Mediation Order Implementation

BACKGROUND

The parents requested a due process hearing to help their son, Mason, with his schoolwork and his problems with speech and learning disabilities. They also want to have vision therapy included as a part of his IEP. Mason is a ten-year-old student eligible for special education and related services as a student with speech language delays and a learning disability. The parents and the district had previously attended mediation on these issues, and the parents, in part, felt the district was not doing its part to uphold the agreement reached. Therefore, the parents requested the due process hearing to receive an order to implement the mediation agreement and to have Mason receive an appropriate education.

The hearing officer stated the following at the beginning of the hearing:

> All discussions that occurred during the mediation process will remain confidential and may not be used as evidence in any subsequent due process hearing or civil procedures as mandated by 300.506 (b)(6)(i) of the Individuals with Disabilities Education Act.

Given that statement, both parties agreed to enter into the record the following statements that they agreed to at the mediation. There were multiple points agreed upon, but the following are specifically in contention:

1. Mason may never lose more than five minutes of daily recess time.
2. The parent will receive a call from the teacher every week to discuss Mason's progress or issues that occurred during the week.

The hearing officer then stated:

> The parties entered into a written mediation agreement. The agreement is valid, legally binding, and enforceable in court. Through the complaint, the parents effectively ask me to enforce the agreement. Just as I have no power to enforce a contract, I have no power to break one either. Since I have no authority to resolve the issue presented in the complaint, or to grant the only relief demanded, I must dismiss this matter for lack of subject matter jurisdiction.

PARENTS' POSITION

The other issues in front of the hearing officer are the parents' demand for the addition of vision therapy in the IEP, incorporating the information from the independent educational evaluation recommendations into his program, and ordering the district to follow the IEP.

In addition to his eligibility for special education and related services as a student with a learning disability and speech needs, Mason has also been diagnosed with strabismus. According to Optometrists Network (n.d.),

> Strabismus, more commonly known as cross-eyed or wall-eyed, is a vision condition in which a person cannot align both eyes simultaneously under normal conditions. One or both of the eyes may turn in, out, up or down. An eye turn may be constant (when the eye turns all of the time) or intermittent (turning only some of the time).[1]

The parents state the strabismus causes significant reading problems, most notably headaches, and Mason does not want to read as a result.

The parents want him to improve, and are requesting vision therapy as a part of his IEP. Specifically, they are requesting optometric vision therapy. Optometric vision therapy is an individualized, supervised, nonsurgical treatment program designed to correct eye movements and visual-motor deficiencies. Vision therapy sessions include procedures designed to enhance the brain's ability to control:

- eye alignment,
- eye teaming,
- eye focusing abilities,
- eye movements, and/or
- visual processing.

---

1. http://www.strabismus.org

The parents stated that if one considers the benefits of in-office therapy combined with school therapy, there is a greater likelihood that Mason he will be more cooperative when he is older.

DISTRICT POSITION

Mason has received supportive services since being initially evaluated in second grade. Mason's most recent evaluation includes a determination of a specific learning disability in the areas of fluency, reading comprehension, and written expression. This reevaluation report yielded the following results:

> On the administration of the WISC-IV, Mason obtained a Full Scale Intelligence Quotient (FSIQ) score of 86, which corresponds to the low average range. On the WIAT-III test Mason scored in the following areas: reading, 76, which falls significantly below a range of expectations; math, 89, which places him within an average range of expectations; written expression, 79, which corresponds to the below average range. On the oral language composite, Mason obtained a score within the average range.

Speech Services

Mason is identified as a student with a speech and language impairment. He currently receives speech therapy services once a week for thirty minutes in a small group setting. His goals have targeted both language processing and articulation skills. Mason's articulation needs are minimal. The only sound in error for Mason is /r/, and he is able to produce this sound with up to 85 percent accuracy during structured tasks when prompted. Additionally, this sound error does not have a significant impact on Mason's overall intelligibility. Mason speaks slowly and clearly and both familiar and unfamiliar listeners easily understand his speech.

The district denies that there has been a denial of FAPE as alleged. Additionally, the parents demand that vision therapy be included as a part of the program is without merit. He is provided reading instruction by a certified special education teacher, and is making progress.

It is the position of the district that in order to respond accurately and effectively to the parents' due process complaint the district would request that the parents provide a more in-depth explanation of the alleged issue surrounding the claims that specific stipulations of the mediation were not followed. Furthermore, it is the district's understanding that the parents have undertaken an independent educational evaluation; however, such results have not been wholly shared with the district so as to give the district a better understanding of the parents' requests. The district understands the parents' claim that they believe Mason's IEP was not adequately followed for their son; however, the parents have failed to identify which provisions, services, or accommodations were not followed or implemented accordingly. Once again, this does not allow the district an opportunity to properly investigate and respond to the allegations within the due process complaint and thus fails in legal sufficiency.

The parents also allege that Mason's grades went down over the course of the academic year; however, directly correlated with this information is the fact that the student missed a lot of classes, both excused and unexcused, throughout the year. The fact that the student missed many of his classes means the district was unable to enter a lot of information on the grades for the student in the grade book. For this reason, the district believes this is not an accurate reflection of the student's performance for the year. Finally, the student was taking medication on a regular basis at lunch. The parents stopped sending in the medication, which created an inconsistency for the student and may have also led to additional performance issues.

Despite what has been alleged by parents, the district is capable of providing educational programming to the student that is appropriate and can provide him with FAPE. The district denies that the IEPs that have been presented this year are incapable of providing Mason with FAPE.

The district has a responsibility to receive, review, and consider the contents of any independent educational evaluation the parents' may request and receive. The district's IEP team is under no obligation to accept wholesale everything that is included in an independent educational evaluation; however, without having the information presented to the district wholly, it becomes nearly impossible to give a true evaluation of the IEE. At this time, to the district's knowledge and belief, the parents reference an IEE report they are relying upon, but they have not wholly shared this document with the district. The district would like to evaluate, consider, and potentially include items from that evaluation report; however, without such information the district is unable to respond. As such, the district believes the student has made meaningful progress over the entire time he has been enrolled in the district.

The district submits that the hearing officers and courts have been consistent that the student's IEP must be looked at during the time the evaluation report was done, and the IEP was developed at that time. The district will be reviewing the mediation agreement with any new teacher of Mason's to ensure that it is fully implemented. The district is also in the midst of scheduling training for general education staff on proper IEP implementation.

Finally, the argument that vision therapy needs to be included is without merit. There is no denial that Mason may have needs related to his strabismus; however, the provider of the training is a certified ophthalmologist, which makes this a medical procedure, and therefore one that the district does not have to provide.

DECISION

The hearing officer applauded both parties for pursing mediation instead of a due process hearing, but understood that differences still remained.

The hearing officer again stated his lack of authority to oversee mediation agreements. Clarifying that this was the responsibility of other compliance authorities.

Regarding the program for vision therapy, the hearing officer found the district was not obligated to provide vision therapy. However, the hearing officer did encourage the parties to work together if Mason did appear exceptionally tired. The hearing officer also affirmed the program and placement for Mason, and did state that it was difficult for him to make progress because he missed so many days (sixty-five during the school year).

Finally, there was no evidence showing the information on the independent educational evaluation should be a part of his educational program. The IEE dealt mostly with vision training.

MASON: SPECIAL EDUCATION
ADMINISTRATOR RESPONSE

In addition to the areas of dispute that are due some discussion is the hearing officer's statement that dismisses the matter of the agreement made in mediation due to lack of jurisdiction. It is important for everyone to understand the intent and purpose of mediation and due process, both of which are required to be options given by the state education agency (SEA) for dispute resolution under IDEA. Neither mediation or due process are required, but both are offered as options. In mediations, both parties must agree to participate, whereas with due process it takes only one party to file. Mediation cannot be used to deny or delay a parent's right to a hearing on a due process complaint. It is important to know that mediation is conducted by a "qualified" impartial mediator. The purpose is to help the parties come to an agreement. This agreement is called a settlement agreement. This agreement is a legally binding agreement and enforceable by a state or district court. However, any settlement agreement must state that "all discussions that occurred during the mediation process will remain confidential and may not be used as evidence in any subsequent due process hearing or civil proceeding" [§300.506(b) (6)(i)]. Therefore, as the hearing officer stated in this case, he is not able to enforce the mediation agreement or consider any statements made during that process. Keep in mind that the benefit of using mediation is that the decision-making power stays with the parties in dispute. The mediator is there to help the parties come to a mutual agreement. This differs from a due process complaint because the hearing officer is the one who makes the decision, based on the facts provided and in accordance with IDEA, as to the findings of the complaint. The parties do not have any say in the decision of the hearing officer. A hearing officer's decisions are final unless the parties choose to appeal the decisions in court.

The other issue for discussion here is focused around the parents' request for the district to pay for a medical service where there is disagreement as to whether service is needed for the student to have access to and make progress in (or benefit from) their special education program. As the facts are presented in this case, an evaluation is referred to as an independent educational evaluation, which is in fact an outside or independent evaluation. There is an important distinction between independent educational evaluations and other evaluations requested by parents. In §300.502 the parental right to request an independent educational evaluation (IEE) is outlined. However, in §300.502(c) it is stated that parents may obtain other evaluations at private expense. Many times the term independent educational evaluation is used to describe both the IEE as defined in §300.502 and what is referred to as "other evaluation parents obtain at private expense." The difference in these two terms is the process to procure the evaluation and the purpose of the evaluation. Families will often have evaluation information that was procured for reasons beyond an educational purpose that included information that would be useful to the IEP team. These evaluations are not payed for by the school district, but when the parents present them, the district is obligated to "consider" the information if "it meets agency criteria, in any decision made with respect to the provision of FAPE" [§300.502(c)(1)]. However, families are not required to give the school district any evaluation information that was obtained at the family's expense.

The process for an independent educational evaluation as outlined in IDEA is very specific. A parent does not have the right to request an IEE until after the school district has conducted their own evaluation and the parent disagrees with the evaluation conducted by the school district. The evaluation information discussed in this case is referring to outside information and not the IDEA process that allows a parent to request an independent education evaluation.

MASON: DISTRICT ATTORNEY RESPONSE

Based on the facts provided in the case study, the hearing officer's decision is based on sound legal principles and is not surprising. The first interesting issue is the interplay between the mediation agreement and the issues before the hearing officer. The decision correctly noted that a hearing officer lacks jurisdiction over the enforcement of a mediation agreement. Arguably, the parents would still have the right to pursue enforcement of a mediation agreement, since Section 300.506(7) provides that, "A written, signed mediation agreement . . . is enforceable in any State court of competent jurisdiction or in a district court of the United States." Therefore, based on a plain reading of the regulation, the hearing officer made the right call regarding jurisdiction. Additionally, the regulations also clearly provided that discussions that occurred during mediation cannot be used as evidence.

The school district raised several important points to support the position that it was not required to provide the optometric vision therapy services for Mason. While the strabismus diagnosis is something the district should not ignore, there seems to be little evidence in this fact pattern to establish that a denial of the therapy is a denial of FAPE. In fact, Mason's scores in fluency, reading comprehension, and written expression do not seem to support the parents' case for the vision therapy. On the contrary, the facts seem to support the hearing officer's conclusion that Mason is making progress in those areas. Similarly, Mason has shown progress in response to speech services.

From the perspective of an attorney representing school districts, it seems very peculiar that the parents are unwilling to share the results of the IEE. Generally, parents are very eager to share those results with a district if they lend strong support for their position. Concealing the IEE results would make most districts and their counsel suspect that the results of the IEE did not lend strong support for the argument that a district failed to provide FAPE. Additionally, the failure to report results or identify the specific problems with the mediation agreement means that both the district and their legal counsel do not have a complete picture on which to base an educational or legal decision involving the case.

Based on the lack of any evidence demonstrating that the vision therapy might be necessary for Mason's education, the facts seem to lend more support that the therapy constitutes medical treatment rather than a service required for FAPE under IDEA. However, despite the result of the hearing officer's decision, the district should probably convene a Section 504 evaluation meeting. While not being required to provide vision therapy services under the IDEA, the strabismus might require accommodations at school under

Section 504 since the parents have stated that condition causes headaches that are affecting Mason's reading.

MASON: PARENT ATTORNEY RESPONSE

Parents often visit an attorney's office armed with evaluations and treatment notes from outside evaluators. They see these outside sources are more trustworthy and skilled at diagnosing the source of their child's concerns. The parents present these documents to us as their best evidence for why they have a case. Then we ask if they shared this information with the school district. Too frequently, the answer is no. If a district reports behaviors of concern or academic struggles, we expect data to support those concerns and a plan to address them. We do not accept a piecemeal unveiling of an evaluation, only revealing information the district thought was helpful. The same must be true for parents.

Here, Mason's parents prevented the district from fully understanding their concerns. Instead of giving the district access to the entire report, they filed a due process complaint to criticize the district for failing to provide appropriate vision services, which was the focus of the IEE. They also did not identify which IEP provisions they felt were not being implemented. Mason's parents did not fulfill their role of sharing important information about Mason with the IEP team. As a result, the district's defense won the day.

However, districts should aim to better understand why parents are hesitant to share information and concerns. Our parents consistently express concerns that information will be used against their child or it will be shared with people who do not need to know about the diagnosis. Keeping the parents involved in the process of how the district will use the information will reduce these concerns.

The district's defense was based on well-reasoned concerns that prevented the IEP team from fully understanding Mason. The hearing officer correctly handled the dispute.

Case Thirteen: Brody

Child Find

BACKGROUND

Brody is a sixteen-year-old boy who enrolled in the district at the beginning of ninth grade. Brody was diagnosed with ADHD in seventh grade and also has diagnoses of depression and anxiety disorder. The parent filed the due process hearing request, seeking compensatory education and other relief due to the failure of the district to offer Brody a free and appropriate public education (FAPE) for two years.

The parent stated that despite having a 504 accommodation plan in place since his arrival in the district, Brody has made minimal academic, emotional, and social progress over the past two school years. Most importantly, he has continued to struggle and regressed to the point that he had to repeat ninth grade. His minimal academic progress was a result of taking the same courses twice, and because he was not provided any appropriate support improvements. Additionally, the manifestations of his ADHD, depression, and anxiety have resulted in numerous disciplinary concerns, from disruption in class to verbal conflicts with teachers and peers.

The parent claimed that this struggle for Brody was compounded by the district's failure to fulfill its child find obligation and request that Brody be reevaluated at the end of the first marking period in his first time through ninth grade. Instead, the parent had to write a letter requesting a psychoeducational evaluation. In that letter, the parent also alerted the district of her concern that Brody had a learning disability and that his struggles were affecting his self-esteem.

The district commenced an evaluation that was returned in October. Thereafter, the district issued an evaluation report in December.

PARENT'S POSITION

The parent claims that the district's evaluation is replete with procedural and substantive violations that ultimately led to a denial of FAPE for the remainder of Brody's attendance due to decisions that were based upon it. First, Brody was referred specifically for a suspected learning disability, yet the "Reason for Referral" section of the report fails to note this request. Second, there was no formal observation in the classroom or other settings to see how Brody functions in different environments. The district was required to complete at least one classroom observation for a child who was referred for a suspected learning disability. Third, for a child who had known behavior difficulties in the classroom, no behavior rating scales were completed. This is a failure to evaluate a child in all areas of suspected disability. Fourth, at the meeting in December to review the results of the evaluation, the evaluating psychologist did not attend.

The parent continued, stating that, based upon the incomplete evaluation, the district staff stated Brody was not qualified for an IEP and he was being offered more of the same 504 accommodation plan. As a result of the district's conclusion, Brody was denied the benefit of an IEP and was relegated to a poorly drafted 504 accommodation plan that lacked any meaningful support that would practically benefit Brody in the classroom. As would be expected, Brody made no academic, emotional, or social progress and, in fact, failed the ninth grade.

The parent continued: Brody's behavior also regressed and he continued to have suspensions after the district's evaluation. Continuing to struggle in school and not getting appropriate help, Brody's motivation and confidence also continued to decline, such that he began to experiment with marijuana and was eventually placed for in-patient treatment by his parent. Brody completed in-patient treatment and has remained drug free ever since. Nevertheless, the district continues to excuse its failures by suggesting drug use.

The parent complained that the district turned a blind eye to Brody's struggles. Brody returned to the district after the in-patient treatment, and again no one requested a meeting to discuss the discharge summary or determine if any additional supports were needed. Although it is not the parent's duty to develop strategies to support and educate Brody, the parent requested that the school counselor check on Brody. The school counselor initially said that he was too busy and that if Brody needed him, he could come see him. This shows the district's fundamental misunderstanding of Brody, as he is not a kid that seeks out help and shifting the burden to him will only result in further decline until he is provided with the skills and support to advocate for himself and become more confident and independent.

Desperate for help, the parent then wrote the principal and asked, for a second time, for an independent evaluation for Brody. The parent reiterated her concern that Brody has a learning disability. The principal denied the request but failed to file for a due process hearing to defend the district's evaluation.

The district failed to file any due process complaint to defend its evaluation; rather, it placed the parent in the position of having to retain legal counsel to secure that which the regulations clearly provide her. With the assistance of counsel retained by the family, the district agreed to fund an evaluation and a partial report was issued to provide the district with initial guidance as quickly as possible in the school year.

The independent evaluator participated in a 504 meeting, where he advised the district that that Brody required an IEP to address his behavioral and emotional needs, which are impacting his learning. The district IEP team rejected his conclusion but requested the family make a proposal for an IEP.

In the meantime, the independent evaluator completed his school observation of Brody and issued his final report in January of Brody's second time in ninth grade. Having all available data now, the independent evaluator made clear that he did not believe Brody's needs could be met with a 504 accommodation plan and that he needed the support of an IEP. The independent evaluator provided clear, specific recommendations to the district, such as that Brody required

> a goal for learning coping skills and strategies and emotional regulation, which should be monitored by the guidance counselor. . . . Additionally, Brody should be taught to advocate for himself in daily situations with his regular education teachers and to generalize those skills to all settings. He should be taught to identify situations where he would need to seek out help and develop a plan to advocate appropriately in those situations.

At a subsequent 504 meeting, the parent, with the assistance of an advocate and legal counsel, explained to the district that based upon the conclusions in the IEE, Brody was eligible for specially designed instruction in coping skills and emotional regulation. The family requested an IEP so that direct instruction could be provided, data could be collected, and Brody's progress could be monitored. The district agreed to provide counseling services but ultimately denied that Brody required an IEP.

Most concerning to the parent is what will happen to Brody when he gets to tenth grade next year and he does not have the executive functioning and emotional regulation skills to handle the stress of a new grade. There is no data to indicate that Brody will fare any better than he did in either ninth grade experience.

Despite a pattern of specific behaviors that resulted in criticism of Brody by teachers, no behavioral analysis was ever conducted by the district to determine the cause and develop a positive behavior support plan for moving forward. As Brody was clearly having some issues, the district should have provided him with the instruction to make better decisions. Instead it has relied on outdated assumptions and generalizations, such as the principal's statement to the parent that "sometimes it's a man thing."

Any doubts that Brody received executive functioning instruction during the school year were resolved over the summer, when Brody repeated the English class that he failed for the second time. First, the district charged the parent for this class and thus did not offer a free education. Second, at only three days into the class, the teacher wrote that he was already in danger of failing and that he

> is rarely on task, even after [she] redirect[s] him to what he should be working on repeatedly. He is not completing the work [they] do in class (which they get credit for based on completion, not accuracy), and has to be reminded of directions and expectations every few minutes. If [the teacher is] not right behind him he is watching videos or wandering around the room instead of even trying the assigned work. He has also been disruptive and loud during silent reading time, refusing to read a book and distracting other students who are reading as required.

Clearly, this was not an appropriate program and setting for Brody because he remains in need of specially designed instruction in emotional regulation, coping skills, and positive behavior management so that he can access the curriculum.

Finally, Brody has not received appropriate support and coaching to manage his ADHD, thus he continues to demonstrate elevated levels of hyperactivity and inattention across settings.

QUESTIONS TO BE ANSWERED

The parent, in filing a due process hearing request, specifically sought the following:

1. a finding that the district has denied Brody a free appropriate public education for two years, specifically by failing to provide direct, explicit, and systematic individual instruction in executive functioning skills and the necessary counseling services to benefit from such instruction,

2. an order that Brody is eligible for an individualized education program and he must be provided with appropriate counseling services and direct instruction in executive functioning, coping skills, and emotional regulation,
3. an award of compensatory education for Brody, to whatever extent necessary to make up for his lost progress and to restore him to the educational path he would have traveled but for the deprivation by the district,
4. an order that the district reimburse the parent for all costs it has imposed on the parent since Brody entered the district, and
5. under Section 504, an order that the district reimburse the parent for the cost of the independent evaluator's professional services when he provides in-person testimony at the due process hearing.

DISTRICT POSITION

The district stated that it did not know Brody had a Section 504 plan when he enrolled, and was not made aware of it until much later. The district also firmly believes that Brody needed to put forth more effort, and also believes that Brody was engaging in ongoing recreational drug use, and that is the reason it failed to acknowledge his disability and to change programming. Additionally, the district stated that it was not obligated to ascertain Brody's disability "at the earliest possible moment."

The district said it provided a reasonable education for a student with a Section 504 plan; however, Brody did not take advantage of this, and therefore caused himself problems.

DECISION

1. The district erred in its determination that Brody is not eligible for special education under the IDEA.
2. Within ten school days of the date of this decision and order, the district shall convene an initial meeting of an IEP team for Brody.
3. The team shall confirm Brody's eligibility for special education.
4. The team shall identify Brody's educational needs and develop an IEP to address them.
5. The private neuropsychologist who conducted the IEE shall be a member of the IEP team for its initial meeting. The cost of that professional's attendance at the IEP meeting shall be at public expense.
6. The IEP team shall also consider whether any additional assessments, including an FBA, are necessary to identify Brody's educational needs.

7. The district failed in its FAPE obligations to Brody under the IDEA and Section 504.
8. The district shall provide Brody with 1,665 hours of compensatory education for the denial of FAPE during both of his years in ninth grade.
9. Within ten school days of the date of this decision and order, the district shall reimburse the parent $750 for the cost of tuition for summer school.

BRODY: SCHOOL DISTRICT ADMINISTRATOR RESPONSE

The district made a number of procedural errors in the evaluation of Brody for special education eligibility. First, they did not complete a classroom observation and second, they did not have the school psychologist attend the evaluation meeting. IDEA clearly outlines the requirement for completing an observation as part of the evaluation process in §300.310, and requires a team member for an evaluation where there is a suspicion of a learning disability. The team member must be someone qualified to conduct individual diagnostic exams under §300.308. The next procedural violation occurred when the parent requested an independent educational evaluation and the principal denied that request. The district has two courses of action it can take when a request for an IEE is made: 1) Provide the parent with information as to where an IEE can be obtained and the agency criteria applicable for an IEE [§ 300.502 (a)(2)], or 2) file for a due process hearing to show that its evaluation is appropriate [§300.502 (b)(2)(i)]. The district did neither.

In her complaint, the parent included concerns with the implementation of the Section 504 plan. However, the dispute resolution process under IDEA does not have authority to address these concerns and is only able to address the IDEA issues. Therefore, the family would need to file a complaint with the Office of Civil Rights in regard to 504 concerns. However, it would be interesting to hear why the district is acknowledging a disability under 504, but not under IDEA. The facts presented here do not go into this detail, but leave one wondering about the consideration of the second prong (demonstrating a need for special education for special education eligibility). A further discussion of the two-prong qualifier for special education warrants further discussion in terms of the independent educational evaluation. Section §300.8(a)(1) discusses what is needed for a team to determine a student is eligible for special education. The student must first meet the criteria of a disability category and second demonstrate a need for special education and related services. This second prong (demonstrating a need for special education) is often an area of conflict among teams in which an IEE has been requested. The IEE will address the criteria for disability categories, and many families and other outside agencies do not realize they need this in addition to the second prong to qualify for an IEP. This second prong is much less black-and-white than the criteria for a disability category.

There also needs to be reference here to the district's child find responsibilities in response to their claim that they did not need to ascertain at the earliest possible moment if Brody had a disability. The IDEA clearly states in the child find regulations that it is the responsibility of the district to locate and evaluate *all* students with a disability within their jurisdiction. The district knew Brody might have a disability when the parent informed them; therefore, they should have conducted an evaluation at that time. There was plenty of evidence Brody possibly had a disability, and based on his lack of progress the district had a very poor argument. It also appears the district did not make any attempts to change Brody's program to increase his success, whether or not his failing was due to ongoing use of recreational drugs. It is interesting the district determined it was appropriate to charge the parent the cost of summer school, especially since there was disagreement about the qualification for special education services. This in light of the fact that education to students with disabilities is provided at no cost to the parents.

BRODY: DISTRICT ATTORNEY RESPONSE

Some of the most adverse results for school districts in special education matters occur as a result of taking a myopic view of a student's behavior by characterizing it solely as a disciplinary matter. This can be especially true in cases involving high school students who have been involved in illegal drug use. When a student has not been previously identified under IDEA, high school administrators may have a tendency to view the legal issues related to that student with the administrators' own bias and experience in dealing with such matters. The principal's comment regarding it being "a man thing" may be an indication that Brody is thought of as a discipline problem without other factors being considered. The facts of this case study indicate that the district seems to be looking past some real red flags indicating the need to evaluate by going straight to a disciplinary solution. While the enforcement of school district policies related to substance abuse is very important, it does not wipe away a district's child find obligations under IDEA.

Because Brody was diagnosed with ADHD in seventh grade and has also been diagnosed with depression and anxiety disorder, it is surprising that Brody does not have an IEP. This is noteworthy because Brody has not shown improvement and the parent has stated that Brody has a suspected learning disability but has not been referred for evaluation. It is also hard to understand why the district would reject the independent evaluator's recommendation at the Section 504 meeting but then ask the parents to make an IEP proposal. This is a flawed approach on two fronts. The first is the fact this is occurring at the 504 meeting instead of through the IDEA. The other issue is that the district should not be improvising by asking the parent to make an IEP proposal. School district clients will sometimes complain about losing control of a special education case. However, in this case study you have a district that takes a "hands-off" approach and offers to allow an IEP proposal without evaluating, effectively ceding their authority as the LEA.

At several points during the timeline of this case study, there were signs that the district needed to evaluate Brody, because he might have a learning disability that requires an IEP. After the ADHD diagnosis, the continued academic struggles into ninth grade should have been additional prompts to evaluate. Additionally, the teacher's observations during summer school clearly identified that Brody was not in an appropriate setting and required specially designed instruction in emotional regulation, coping skills, and positive behavior management.

It is not surprising that the decision went against the district since it would be hard to argue that the district met child find obligations. However, it would seem more appropriate for the district to be ordered to conduct an evaluation for the purposes of IDEA prior to ordering an IEP team to meet or develop an IEP. The decision to allow the private neuropsychologist to make a determination of qualification appears odd when it seems evident the district has not been involved enough in the evaluation and probable development of an IEP. The award of 1,665 hours of compensatory education seems incomplete until there is some determination of what level of service should have been provided in the previous two years. Finally, the award of $750 for the cost of tuition for summer school is basically a money damages award, which is inappropriate under the IDEA.

Although the hearing officer's decision is full of legal flaws, districts that brush aside signs that a student needs to be evaluated under the IDEA run the risk of a decision that is ultimately a good deal more burdensome than the cost of services they would have provided had the student been identified early on.

BRODY: PARENT ATTORNEY RESPONSE

While it is not an issue identified or addressed in Brody's case, after reviewing the background I am most concerned about the future delivery of FAPE for Brody. The facts show a broken IEP team focused on playing the blame game instead of problem-solving. Although this dispute is over, the team will still need to plan for Brody's education well into the future. While the decision gives some guidance on how to move forward, it does little to create a cohesive team to support Brody in the future.

The failure of the IEP team is on display regarding Brody's drug use. The parent argued that Brody completed in-patient treatment and was now drug free. Yet the district continued to blame the drug use for Brody's lack of progress. The district did so without any meeting to discuss the discharge summary or determine if any additional supports were needed. When the parent requested help from the counselor, the district placed all the responsibility for a successful intervention on Brody. The team never had an opportunity to effectively communicate about Brody's drug use and how they might support each other moving forward. Brody was labeled as a drug user and the district refused to show empathy or understanding for this struggle. Had they done so, the outcome may have been different.

Attorneys representing parents should focus on continuing to work with a school district beyond the issuance of a decision to solve problems, no matter the result of the decision. One saying we use to attempt to frame the need to come together after a dispute is "Here we are." By accepting the concept of "here we are," the team hopefully can answer the question "Where do we need to go next?" Instead of lingering in the past, and on who was right or wrong, we accept the fact that we need to implement the order and move forward as a team. Ideally, both the parent and district will put their egos aside and focus on this goal. This can often occur with the assistance of an IEP Facilitator.

IEP facilitation is the same as any other IEP meeting, except that a trained facilitator joins the meeting. This individual helps with communication between team members but does not make decisions about the student's IEP. Facilitators are skilled at modeling effective communication and listening. Their goal is to improve relationships among team members and assist in resolving disagreements. Unfortunately, IEP facilitation is not available in every state and is not required under the IDEA. Luckily, a viable alternative exists.

LEAs should consider assigning one IEP team member to be the parent advocate. Their role is to make sure the parent understands what is being proposed and has all their questions answered. Instead of only reporting how Brody behaves in his particular class, the LEA parent advocate focuses on obtaining parental support for the decisions of the team. This will also give the parent comfort and allow them to be more open with the team. As a result, the team learns more about how to best educate the student.

Too often the focus is on obtaining the parent's "yes" to the district's plan. This "yes" is often a meaningless way for the parent to escape a lengthy meeting about topics they don't understand. This "yes" does nothing to shore up the district's defenses against a due process hearing. Instead of obtaining a cheap yes, an IEP team's focus must remain on creating a cohesive team that understands the path to achieving the annual goals. A parent's comment of "that's right" instead of "yes" makes a huge difference. This can only happen when the parent has buy-in and engagement in the IEP process. Once they can take ownership of the ideas contained in the IEP, due process is the last thought on a parent's mind.

Case Fourteen: Destiny

Section 504

BACKGROUND

Destiny is a fifteen-year-old student eligible for special education and related services under the classification of specific learning disabilities due to reading comprehension, decoding, and fluency issues. She is also eligible under the category of other health impairment due to a diagnosis of Ehlers-Danlos syndrome (hypermobility type).

PARENTS' POSITION

The parents filed a due process hearing, alleging the IEP was insufficient and inappropriate to meet Destiny's academic, medical, and behavioral needs. The parents allege she was blatantly discriminated against and singled out due to a behavior that should have been addressed through her IEP. She was singled out, as were others, by having to wear a green shirt when her homework was not handed in, a manifestation of her disability. Specifically, the parents allege that staff made derogatory comments due to her race and disability and she was demoralized by her teachers for her lack of academic success. The parents went further, stating her behaviors were not addressed through a functional behavior assessment and behavior support plan. The parents also allege her IEP did not contain goals/objectives and special accommodations to meet her overall needs, causing her a deprivation of educational benefits.

When Destiny started in the district at grade seven, she had a Section 504 plan that the parents also allege was not implemented by the district. Destiny was diagnosed with Ehlers-Danlos syndrome (hypermobility type) prior to being evaluated by the district. The parents reported that they continually told the district that there was something not right with their child's education and pled with them until they finally did an evaluation. The parents were, in part, demanding an evaluation due to Destiny failing all of her classes. Additionally, the parents continued to receive comments and notes from the teachers indicating that Destiny was excessively tired in class—she either had her head down or was sleeping, and was increasingly argumentative. As a result of the parents' demands, the district completed an evaluation. For their part, the parents stated that their biggest concern was Destiny getting her homework in on time. Specifically, the parents noted that Destiny will complete the homework but not turn it in. There was nothing in the evaluation addressing homework completion.

Statements from the teachers include:

1. Destiny's participation is far below her peers. I am most concerned with consistent homework completion and maintaining on-task performance.
2. Destiny is a quick learner and often participates in class. I'm most concerned with work completion and test/quiz scores.
3. Destiny needs a reinforcement system for work completion.

As a result of the evaluation, the district developed an IEP to help Destiny with her learning disabilities. The district noted as a part of this IEP that Destiny does not exhibit behaviors that impede her learning or that of others. The discipline logs state the following for the first half of eighth grade: "There are thirty-seven infractions, including defiance, disrespect and lateness to class." The notes home to the parents indicted Destiny's actions of putting her head down on her desk and sleeping as defiance. The medication she takes causes her to be severely tired.

As a result of the frequent behavioral problems, the district had the parents and Destiny sign a behavioral contract which stated:

> *If your unprofessional behavior continues and you exceed ten write-ups while on this behavior contract for a nine-week marking period, more severe consequences may occur which may include suspension and a probation contract.*

Additionally, as a result of her problems with homework completion, she was required to wear a green shirt if completion fell below 80 percent. This was a districtwide practice. Destiny had to wear a green shirt the entire year. There was no plan to change her behavior or to help her with homework completion. It was reported that students wearing the green shirts were targeted and bullied during lunch. Destiny also noted that her English teacher would take her into the hallway and tell her she was dumb and stupid.

The parents also allege the IEP was deficient. Specifically, the goals and objectives in the IEP were either nonexistent or not sufficient enough in scope to address her medical issues, homework issues, and the significant discrepancy between her cognitive ability and measured reading skills of decoding, fluency, and comprehension.

As a result of the problems with the IEP, and the lack of supports provided to her, Destiny failed eighth grade. The main reason she failed was due to lack of homework completion, which for some of her classes accounted for up to 30 percent of her grade.

In filing this due process hearing, the parents are requesting the following:

1. Compensatory education for the seventh and eighth grade school years for the entire time she attended
2. An order that Destiny receive credit for eighth grade and be allowed to move on to ninth grade.

DISTRICT POSITION

The district's response will be divided into four parts. Part One is a discussion of the 504 plan. Part Two is a discussion of the evaluation report. Part Three is a summary of the evaluation.

Part One

The Section 504 plan is appropriate. Specifically, the following are accommodations provided to Destiny:

1. Tap Destiny's desk if needed to remind her about her posture.
2. Allow Destiny to take notes on a laptop during English.
3. Permit Destiny to complete her written work while leaning on a binder to provide support.
4. Permit Destiny into class if she shows her late pass.
5. Permit Destiny to do finger exercises for five to ten minutes in class to reduce joint pain.
6. Allow Destiny to complete a test after school if she was unable to complete it during class due to joint pain or fatigue.
7. Permit Destiny to wear warm clothing.
8. Permit Destiny to take a break during prolonged periods of sitting.
9. Provide rest breaks if Destiny is having trouble keeping up with her peers.
10. Assign fewer problems/reduced workload so Destiny can show mastery of the skill while minimizing fatigue.

The 504 plan is individually tailored to the needs presented by her, and has clear directives for the teachers, for the 504 plan coordinator, for school administrators, for Destiny, and for Destiny's parents. The 504 plan was developed with Destiny's needs in mind and provides her accommodations necessary to participate in a general education classroom. The accommodations listed are the ones that a school should reasonably provide to a student with this condition.

Part Two

The district commenced an evaluation of Destiny.

She started eighth grade not eligible for special education and related services. It is reasonable for a school to not be expected to initiate a referral for an evaluation report until the student starts to have problems in school. The school waited until the end of the first marking period, and given her low grades initiated testing for special education eligibility. Her grades were so low that she failed all her subjects. Teachers also noted that she is excessively tired in class, often putting her head down, and stated that she engages in argumentative behavior and work refusal.

Part Three

Summary from the Evaluation

Based on the information from the evaluation report, Destiny qualified for specially designed instruction under the educational classification of Specific Learning Disability (reading decoding, comprehension, and fluency) and Other Health Impairment due to her diagnosis of Ehlers-Danlos syndrome. It was recommended that goals be put into place to address reading deficits as well as work completion. Additionally, accommodations from Destiny's 504 plan should be adopted into her IEP, and Destiny should also receive accommodations and modifications to address deficits in working memory and processing speed.

The district completed a very thorough and detailed evaluation of Destiny. The district looked at multiple measures, received input from her parents, and found her eligible for special education and related services. It is clear Destiny has problems with reading, and the tests indicate the need for assistance in this area. The recommendations are individualized, completed within the state mandated timelines, included the appropriate personnel, and fully consider all the areas of need. The evaluation is strong and was completed appropriately.

However, the district acknowledges that the IEP can be improved. The district welcomes an opportunity to meet with the parents to do so.

DECISION

It is hereby ordered that:

1. The accommodations in the 504 plan were provided appropriately.
2. The school did not discipline the student inappropriately.
3. The parent was not denied meaningful participation in developing the IEP.
4. The school's not promoting the student to tenth grade was appropriate.
5. The behavior contract accompanying the 504 plan was not appropriate.
6. The IEP was not appropriate in the areas of behavior support, reading instruction, and instruction in executive functioning.
7. As the school denied the student FAPE under Section 504 and the IDEA, the student is entitled to compensatory education as follows:

    a) 504 Behavior Contract and IEP Behavior Plan: 30 minutes (0.5 hours) per day for every day the student was present in school from November through the last day of school in June of eighth grade
    b) IEP Reading: 45 minutes (0.75 hours) for every day the student was present in school from April through the last day of school in June of eighth grade
    c) IEP Executive Functioning: 45 minutes (0.75 hours) for every day the student was present in school from April through the last day of school in June of eighth grade
    d) These hours are to be used for direct reading instruction, direct instruction in executive functioning skills, psychoeducational counseling, or any other relevant service or program that addresses the student's areas of need.
    e) The parent may use the hours to purchase services at the usual and customary rate for private providers of these services in [the local area] and/or the counties geographically adjacent to [the local area].
    f) The hours may be used after school, on weekends, and/or in the summer until the student reaches age 21.

DESTINY: SPECIAL EDUCATION
ADMINISTRATOR RESPONSE

This case clearly demonstrates where a districtwide practice can be discriminatory against students with disabilities. In this particular case, it had to do with homework completion. Districts need to review their policies and consider practices that may discriminate against a particular population. Many students with disabilities have difficulty with organization and completion of work, which is a manifestation of their disability, and therefore punishing them for this would be a discriminatory practice.

The district's defense of the 504 plan stating the accommodations provided are ones that are reasonable for a student with this particular condition is not in keeping with the intent of the regulations. When a student with a disability is not being successful with what is outlined in a 504 plan, the district has the responsibility to consider if that student would need special education and related services to receive FAPE. The district also stated they did not need to initiate an evaluation until a student was having difficulty. This is not congruent with the IDEA regulations. In §300.111, the child find regulations, it clearly states that the district is required to locate, identify, and evaluate any student with a disability living in their jurisdiction.

Therefore, when a district suspects a student has a disability, they must move forward with the process to evaluate and identify. In this case the district clearly had reason to suspect Destiny had a disability based on the fact that that she had a medical diagnosis as well as a 504 plan. This regulation is another area in which districts and families have indications, and it is not clear as to what constitutes a "suspicion" of a disability under IDEA. This comes from the fact that to be identified as a student with a disability under IDEA a student must meet the criteria for one of the disability categories *and* require special education. Often it is assumed by families and others that if a student has a diagnosed disability they qualify for an IEP, not being aware of the second prong needed for special education services. Schools often make the mistake of thinking a student must fail to qualify for an IEP. Both of these presumptions are inaccurate and communication needs to happen between families and schools to work through these issues and meet the needs of the student as intended by the law.

In this case, the district should have commenced an evaluation when Destiny starting showing problems with her behavior to determine if those behaviors were a manifestation of the disability and needed to be addressed for her to have access to and make progress in the curriculum. The grades and work completion were another red flag the team should have considered earlier to determine if changes to her program needed to be made. Another error the district made was in terms of the homework completion. When the evaluation was eventually completed, the evaluation team made recommendations that work completion be addressed, and according to the facts this was left out of the developed IEP. This could lead to the assumption the IEP was not reasonably calculated to provide FAPE. It is important to keep in mind that when a student with a disability is not being successful, for whatever reason, the team needs to make sure they have taken due diligence in working to identify why, make changes to the program, and have the data available to support the decision or recommendations that are made.

DESTINY: DISTRICT ATTORNEY RESPONSE

The facts underlying Destiny's case constitute legal exposure for the district that goes beyond concerns regarding appropriate evaluation or the development of IEPs and Section 504 plans. There are some examples of issues that may lead to an allegation of discriminatory conduct under federal law. One issue that should get the attention of the district is the diagnosis of Ehlers-Danlos syndrome. Whenever a student has been diagnosed with a serious health condition, schools should not limit their response to making a determination of eligibility under Section 504. There should be some effort to determine what accommodations the student will require as a follow-up. Unfortunately, due in part to the broad definition of a disability under the Americans with Disabilities Act and Section 504, districts have to be mindful about making sure the 504 plan provides reasonable accommodations. Under these facts, the 504 plan hardly seems to provide accommodations at all. It is surprising to read that Destiny's posture is identified as an issue but there seems to be zero consideration of whether occupational therapy, different seating, or other accommodations might work. Another example is that because Destiny requires finger exercises for joint pain, one has to wonder why the district did not request permission to evaluate her to determine if occupational therapy might be necessary.

It is also surprising that the district is labeling any student with a specific shirt color for failing to turn in homework, especially students with disabilities. Most parent attorneys would seize on this kind of labeling as an example of blatant discrimination. The district would be vulnerable to that allegation because the shirt color has resulted in Destiny being bullied at school. The number of disciplinary infractions would also be troubling for an attorney trying to defend the district, especially when the student is being cited for "defiance" for putting her head down or sleeping. After reviewing a lot of disciplinary policies, I would be surprised if Destiny's conduct really violated the district's disciplinary policies. Moreover, discipline for that type of behavior strikes me as oddly heavy-handed. Because Destiny is being disciplined for behavior that might be due to her physical condition, this creates additional fodder for a possible discrimination claim against the district. Finally, the district's failure to conduct a manifestation review before threatening to suspend Destiny is a legally flawed approach.

Despite the learning disability, it sounds as if the major teacher complaints regarding participation, staying on task, and failing to turn in work should be examined to determine what kinds of supports might be effective in dealing with those problems. Because teachers have identified the need for a reinforcement system for completion, it is hard to understand why the district did not address that concern. The hearing officer's decision seems reasonable regarding the award of compensatory education. However, from a school district attorney's perspective, the expectation that a parent will effectively spend the money in the areas identified for compensatory education seems like wishful thinking. It is also surprising that the hearing officer concluded the accommodations in the Section 504 Plan were appropriate since they hardly seem to address the physical challenges Destiny seems to be facing at school.

DESTINY: PARENT ATTORNEY RESPONSE

The IDEA is an antidiscrimination statute as much as an education statute. The statute makes this clear in its first section: The purpose of the act is to recognize that disability is a natural part of the human experience and in no way diminishes the right to participate in or contribute to society and receive an education (20 USC § 1400). Before its enactment, children with disabilities did not receive appropriate educational services, and were excluded from public school and their peers. The facts of this case show our education system has not completely escaped its discriminatory past.

I am struck by the use of a green shirt to signal that homework was not being completed. It is akin to a dunce cap or scarlet letter. With regulations that dictate positive rather than negative behavior intervention, how did this practice get past the numerous educated adults that had to be too involved in its implementation? It is demeaning and ineffective. It is not surprising that an LEA that used shaming to shape behavior also lacked an understanding of how Destiny's behaviors interfere with her learning.

The IDEA requires IEP teams to consider whether behavior is interfering with learning when developing an IEP. As a parent attorney, I use a broad definition of behavior when reviewing records for a potentially unaddressed need. B. F. Skinner, whose work shapes much of the theory behind FBAs (functional behavior assessments) and PBSPs (positive behavior support plans), supports this approach. He defined behavior as "what an organism is doing or more accurately what it is observed by another organism to be doing." There is no label of bad or good behavior, just observations. Many LEAs I have interacted with only consider interfering behavior when a student has numerous disciplinary referrals.

Here, I wonder what the IEP team truly considered when asked if behavior was interfering with Destiny's learning. She had a behavior contract! Children's problematic behaviors are often symptoms of disabilities. It is the job of the adults in the child's life to teach the child to manage these symptoms and provide more healthy replacement behaviors. If we fail to do so, there is an enormous social cost to society.

I am surprised the LEA did not face a harsher order.

Case Fifteen: Amelia

Compensatory Education

BACKGROUND

This is a child find claim requesting compensatory education under the Individuals with Disabilities Education Act, 20 U.S.C. §1401 *et seq.* (IDEA) and the Rehabilitation Act of 1973, 29 U.S.C. §794 (Section 504). Amelia attended the elementary school in the district from kindergarten through third grade.

Beginning in kindergarten, Amelia demonstrated behavioral needs in school. She had a difficult transition to school, which did not improve as the year progressed. Her parents were frequently called to school for meetings about Amelia's behavior. Due to the teacher's concerns, Amelia's parents had her medically evaluated and they learned she had ADHD. During kindergarten Amelia's mother informed the school of the ADHD diagnosis. Teacher comments on her kindergarten and first grade report cards indicated that she was off-task, disrupted other students, and was uncooperative. Homework was not completed on time. Amelia also had a significant number of absences: 31 days in kindergarten and 20.5 days in first grade. Some of these absences resulted when her parents were told to pick up Amelia at school and bring her home due to behaviors she exhibited.

During second grade, Amelia continued to demonstrate problematic behavior. Her teachers indicated that her progress would improve if her behavior was better. Amelia continued to be off-task. She failed to complete homework on time. She needed to improve recall of math facts. She disrupted class, and was uncooperative and disrespectful. Despite the same ongoing concerns and its knowledge that Amelia had ADHD, the district still failed to initiate an initial evaluation. In March of second grade the district offered Amelia a support group, which was a lunch bunch facilitated by a guidance counselor. No other services were put in place for Amelia.

During third grade, Amelia spiraled downward behaviorally and academically. She continued to exhibit problematic behaviors, beginning in the fall with an incident on the school bus and continuing through June when she reportedly assaulted a substitute teacher. The district's records indicated behavioral concerns included violations of school policies, leaving the classroom without permission, disturbing other students, and refusal to do work. In February, she reportedly punched a teacher on one occasion and hit a peer during another incident. The district responded with out-of-school suspensions, six of which were formally documented as discipline. On many other days her parents were called and told that they needed to pick Amelia up because she was suspended, though these incidents were not documented as discipline. Although her parents told the principal that Amelia's behaviors resulted from her ADHD diagnosis, the district did not initiate an evaluation process, offer a positive behavior support plan, or take action to help her. Amelia missed a total of 22.5 days during third grade, many of which were exclusions from school. Her schoolwork suffered and was inconsistent throughout third grade, and as a result she had erratic grades in all subjects.

Recognizing that Amelia was failing miserably, her parents enrolled her in a charter school for fourth grade, where she was soon provided with a Section 504 accommodation plan to address her ADHD. Later in the year, after completing an initial evaluation, the charter school found Amelia IDEA eligible under an other health impairment (OHI) classification due to her ADHD and provided her with services to address her emotional and behavioral needs as well as weakness in math fluency.

PARENTS' POSITION

Amelia's parents allege her rights were violated and their daughter should have been receiving specialized services during her tenure in the district. The parents' claims were within the statutory filing period pursuant, and they are entitled to seek a remedy for Amelia dating back to first grade, by which time the district should have conducted an initial evaluation. The parents complaint alleges that the District ignored many indicators that are the hallmark of a student with behavioral needs who has a disability and Amelia was not able to make appropriate gains academically, emotionally, and behaviorally in the district's programming without specialized services in place. The parents claim there was no programming to help Amelia with emotional and behavioral regulation, or to help her stay on task and comply with expectations. Finally, they claim that she did not have adequate access to the curriculum and was fully excluded from educational programming on days when the district sent her home due to her behaviors.

PROPOSED RESOLUTION

Amelia's parents seek the following relief in resolution of her claims:

1. compensatory education for the district's failure to provide Amelia with FAPE during the kindergarten, first, and second grade school years, and
2. reimbursement for the attorney's fees and costs the family will incur in the prosecution of this complaint.

DISTRICT POSITION

The district notes that in third grade Amelia missed approximately sixty-one days of school; thirty-six through a host of excused absences, vacations, deaths of immediate family members; and an additional twenty-five days for early dismissals in which the student left with three or four periods remaining each day. The parents attempted to state that many of those days were as a result of evaluations; however, the fact remains the student missed a lot of school.

Amelia had a lot of disciplinary problems:

1. One-day suspension for assaulting a teacher
2. One-day suspension for refusing to participate in state testing, walking out, and roaming the halls
3. One-day suspension for use of the "N" word and hiding
4. One-day suspension for refusing to do classwork, walking around the room disturbing other students, and when confronted, punching the teacher
5. One-day suspension for pouring perfume in another student's water bottle
6. Violated computer use policy by using another student's password and changing their account information. While being investigated, Amelia left the classroom without permission.
7. Throwing food on the bus

Kindergarten Teacher

Amelia's kindergarten teacher stated she doesn't recall the parents being called to meetings regarding their child's behavior. She does not recall any mention of ADHD diagnosis. She admitted there were comments on report cards about being off-task, disruptive, and uncooperative. However, she believed there was not a need to refer Amelia for any services. She outlined the behavior that was described above was indicative of the types of behavior you would see in an all-day kindergarten. She stated that Amelia exhibited a lack of maturity, was the baby of her family, and was young to begin kindergarten, but the teacher wasn't sure of Amelia's birth date. She was asked if she was aware if Amelia had any early childhood education or Head Start, and she believes Amelia may have been involved in Head Start.

First Grade Teacher

Amelia's first grade teacher confirmed that Amelia exhibited problematic behaviors, but she enjoyed having her. Amelia was very active. The teacher recalls lots of conferences with Amelia's mother in which they discussed movement and being off-task. However, the teacher outlined that if Amelia was asked a question she could answer it. The teacher indicated there was constant communication with the parents, including phone calls and emails. The parents attended spring and fall conferences. The teacher commented that students at this young age can be very active, and can even fall out of chairs. She indicated that she encourages movement. She stated she didn't have a stationary classroom, and that she had no problem with students sitting on the floor while reading was occurring. She was specifically asked if she recalls anything about ADHD, and commented, "Mom may have said ADHD in first grade, but there was no medical information." The teacher communicated that she did not have any academic concerns with Amelia's performance. She commented that the registration packet may have some insight as to whether there was any reference to ADHD.

Second Grade Teacher

Amelia's second grade teacher confirmed that Amelia would present as being uncooperative, stubborn, apathetic, disrespectful, and off-task. She also confirmed Amelia did not complete her homework. She stated that in discussions with Amelia's parents, the parents said she refused to do it. She said she would make a homework station and have Amelia do her homework in the morning when she arrived for school. The teacher doesn't recall whether mom or dad mentioned ADHD in second grade. She does recall Amelia's parents said that Amelia refused to do homework at home. She stated she believed there was no reason to refer Amelia for an evaluation. She did not believe Amelia's behaviors were impeding her education.

Third Grade Teacher

Amelia's third grade teacher stated there were a lot of volatile situations in the classroom. As it relates to the suspensions that occurred in third grade, she stated that a lot happened on the playground, in the cafeteria, or with substitute teachers. She does recall Amelia using the "N" word. She clarified that Amelia is white, not African American. She stated that Amelia's home life was extremely bad, and that she didn't have time to give Amelia attention. She stated there were a lot of students with emotional disturbance in her classroom. For example, three kids were put into outside placements from her classroom and these kids arrived around the holidays. Once again, this teacher was also unsure whether Amelia's ADHD was mentioned.

School Counselor

She was asked what her recollections were as they related to the ADHD issue. She recalls receiving a call from a caseworker and that eventually a behavioral specialist came in on one or two occasions in kindergarten. She stated that the behavioral specialist came from a mental health agency. She stated that she never received any paperwork from the parents or the agency that sent the behavioral specialist. She said that she asked for the paperwork from the parents. When asked if Amelia's mom made any mention in writing or verbally stating she was disgusted with the school, she and others had no recollection of that being said. The school counselor stated that the principal would call Amelia's mom to discuss situations with her, but the mother would just hang up the phone. As it relates to the allegation that Amelia's dad was asked to simply come and pick up the child, the school counselor confirmed it was not done that way. She confirmed that at the time of the mental health agency person coming in she apprised the principal of the situation.

DECISION

1. The district denied FAPE to Amelia from January of kindergarten until the last day third grade.
2. The district shall provide the student with five hours of compensatory education for every day school was in session from January of first grade through the end of third grade.

Within thirty days of the date of this order, the district shall convene a meeting of the student's IEP team to revise the student's IEP, develop a PBSP based on existing information, and plan for an FBA at the start of the school year.

AMELIA: SPECIAL EDUCATION
ADMINISTRATOR RESPONSE

The facts presented by the parents in this case would lead the reader to believe the district clearly suspected that Amelia was a child with a disability and the district erred in not identifying her. When a student is having significant behavioral issues and classroom interventions are not helping to improve those behaviors, steps should be taken to determine if the student has a disability. It appears that in Amelia's case her grades were intermittently adequate and that there was not total failure across the board. However, one could argue she had the ability to perform, as demonstrated when her grades were good, but there was something getting in the way when they were not. As the facts are presented, it does not appear the district implemented any behavioral interventions. It is a common practice in schools to send students home when they have behaviors that are not acceptable and are disrupting the learning of others. Staff needs to be aware of the rights of students when it comes to disciplinary removals. IDEA allows for a district to withhold educational services from students with disabilities for up to ten days each school year without further actions. However, at that point it is considered a "change of placement," and there are specific steps that need to be taken. In this case the team did not get to that point because the district failed to identify Amelia as a student with a disability. However, the practice of sending students home when they are displaying problematic behaviors warrants discussion and concern.

The facts presented in this case made brief mention that the parents' complaint was made within the statutory filing period. This is outlined in §300.507(a)(2), which states that

> the due process complaint must allege a violation that occurred not more than two years before the date the parent or public agency knew or should have known about the alleged action that forms the basis of the due process complaint, or, if the State has an explicit time limitation for filing a due process complaint under this part, in the time allowed by that State law.

Therefore, the timeline for filing a due process complaint is two years after the actions that are the source of the complaint or from the date the complainant should have known the problem happened, unless an individual state has a separate timeline.

One might question in this case why the hearing officer awarded compensatory education for three years. The family realized she should have been evaluated when they took her to the charter school and she was identified and services implemented that improved her educational performance. Therefore, the two years began then. The compensatory services were awarded for the time she did not receive appropriate services because of the district's failure to evaluate and serve her as a student with a disability. It is important to know your state's due process complaint process and other early dispute resolution options offered. All states must offer mediation; however, some go above and beyond this and will offer other options such as IEP facilitation.

AMELIA: DISTRICT ATTORNEY RESPONSE

Because there were so many dropped balls and missed cues in this case study, it is hard to know where to begin. The district's legal position in this case is severely compromised by the number of missed signs showing that Amelia should have been evaluated. The information provided by educators from the district also reveals a lack of proper documentation and an inability to recall whether certain issues were raised with any degree of certainty.

The first sign of problems occurred in kindergarten. The allegation of the parents that the district was aware of Amelia's ADHD seems credible when paired with the behaviors she was exhibiting, which included being off-task and disruptive to other students. The kindergarten teacher, like others in the district, was not able to recall whether the district was put on notice about the ADHD diagnosis. This would suggest to a hearing officer that the district was very neglectful in their documentation. The "I don't recall" defense about the student's diagnosis undermines the credibility of educators and would play very poorly in a hearing. A district is in a much stronger position regarding notice issues if it can assert that such a diagnosis would have been documented in the district's records and that no such record exists. Repeated instances of uncertainty about that issue may lead to a conclusion that the district was disengaged and unconcerned about child find obligations.

Even assuming that the district was not aware of the ADHD diagnosis, it would have been advisable for the district to evaluate Amelia before moving in the direction of severe discipline. Whenever a school district client starts considering exclusion from class as a disciplinary option for children in lower grades, my first set of questions usually focuses on what measures have been tried to deal with the behavior and whether the behavior warrants an evaluation under IDEA. School districts also have to be mindful of avoiding evaluating a student due to rationalizations based on transition to kindergarten or the birth order of a child. Sometimes there is a tendency to avoid early evaluation of students. Such avoidance seldom turns out well for districts if a student continues to struggle, especially if it is evident that a student should have been evaluated. The problem with trying to assess whether the disciplinary issues that first appeared in kindergarten were manifestations of a disability is that the district never evaluated Amelia. Finally, the district's response to the parents' claims actually makes a case for evaluation. The facts also seem to emphasize a real need for a positive behavior support plan.

It is not surprising that the hearing officer would award five hours of compensatory education every day school was in session from first through third grade. However, like many of the other decisions, I am troubled by the lack of specificity regarding what the compensatory education will include. It is also hard to understand why the district will convene and revise the student's IEP when the charter school should be recognized as the current LEA. However, I recognize this view is not shared by a number of courts.

AMELIA: PARENT ATTORNEY RESPONSE

Most parents have experienced a time when they are shocked into a realization that their child is growing up quickly. Their son or daughter may look particularly grown up in a picture or say something beyond their perceived abilities. We are so focused on trying to work through the everyday challenges of parenting that we ignore the bigger picture. Only a strong outside stimulus can shake us from our tunnel vision. Child find claims often materialize in the same way.

Here, Amelia's teachers were caught up in the moment and did not take the opportunity to review what was becoming a clear history of the general education curriculum not working for this student. This often occurs because teachers naturally compensate for weaknesses and differentiate instruction to make sure learning occurs. Their tolerance level for the amount of work necessary to teach a struggling student without a written plan is often too high. It is difficult for the teachers to take a step away from the day-to-day and look at the bigger picture.

Conversely, child find claims are often the easiest to evaluate as a parent attorney. When a parent comes to us, we examine a child's entire educational history with the goal of identifying issues. We have the benefit of examining what the LEA knew or should have known as a whole. After reviewing the records, it is easy to conclude if an LEA should have requested an evaluation. There are common "red flags" we look for when evaluating potential claims that may not be readily apparent to a teacher stuck in the moment.

Here, Amelia's educational record reflects numerous red flags. Amelia had frequent absences, which included numerous requests by the school to have her parents pick her up. Her consistent behavior concerns eventually elevated to an assault on a teacher. Six suspensions are excessive for a third-grader.

Finally, her academic performance was sporadic, indicating Amelia could succeed but her behavior was severely limiting her ability to do so.

While the teachers testified that they did not see a reason to refer Amelia for an evaluation, I hope they changed their approach moving forward for other students. The record here reflects a child in need of additional supports and services. The failure to provide them resulted in a costly decision for the LEA.

LEAs should also take note of the remedy ordered by the hearing officer. The compensatory education was not limited to days Amelia was in attendance. Rather, Amelia was awarded five hours of compensatory education for *every* day school was in session. While the LEA attempted to use the absences as part of their defense, the hearing officer correctly found that the absences were another manifestation of the LEA's failure to provide appropriate support.

The IDEA does not treat school attendance as a parent problem. Special education does not start and stop at the school doors. LEAs must make efforts to have all students comply with compulsory attendance laws, but also consider what additional steps and specially designed instruction should be provided to children with disabilities. When a child's absences are connected with a disability-related need, the LEA should consider conducting an evaluation.

About the Authors

DAVID BATEMAN, SHIPPENSBURG UNIVERSITY

David Bateman is a professor in the Department of Educational Leadership and the Department of Special Education at Shippensburg University of Pennsylvania. He has a BA in government and foreign affairs from the University of Virginia, an MEd in special education from the College of William and Mary, and a PhD in special education from the University of Kansas. He was a due process hearing officer for the Commonwealth of Pennsylvania for close to 600 due process hearings. He is the coauthor of *A Principal's Guide to Special Education, Third Edition*, and the *Special Education Program Administrator's Handbook*. From 2007–2010 he had a due process case study column for the journal *Teaching Exceptional Children*.

JENIFER CLINE, GREAT FALLS SCHOOL DISTRICT

Jenifer Cline is the unit manager for continuing education and technical assistance in the Office of Public Instruction for the state of Montana. She is the former student services coordinator in the Great Falls Public School District in Great Falls, Montana. She received both her BA and MA in speech and hearing sciences from Washington State University and practiced speech pathology in the public schools for six years. She then worked as the director of the Sanders County Special Education Services Cooperative (of Montana) for seven years. She currently serves as the past president of the Montana Council of Administrators of Special Education and remains active in the national Council of Administrators of Special Education. She is the coauthor of *A Teacher's Guide to Special Education*, published by the Association for

Supervision & Curriculum Development (ACSD); *Using Data to Improve Student Learning*, published by National Professional Resources, Inc.; and *Effective and Efficient Management of Resources*, part of the CASE Special Education Leadership Monograph Series, published by the Council for Administrators of Special Education.

WITH

Jonathan Steele, Esq.

He is a graduate of the Duquesne University School of Law. Jonathan also holds a degree in music education from Youngstown State University. Prior to attending law school, Jonathan worked as an elementary music educator. He is a member of the Pennsylvania Bar and has been admitted to the United States District Court for the Western District of Pennsylvania.

Sean Fields, Esq.

Sean is a graduate of the Dickinson School of Law of Penn State University and Northern Kentucky University. He currently serves as an adjunct professor at Shippensburg University in the Department of Educational Leadership and as a member of the Shippensburg University School Study Council. Sean currently writes and edits a monthly newsletter called *CGA School Law Snapshot*.

Made in the USA
Monee, IL
19 August 2022

11987709R00083